*Best
Basketball
Booster*

25
14

Best
Basketball
Booster

by S. C. Lee

DESIGN BY KARL SCOTT
PHOTOGRAPHS BY SANTIAGO RIVERA

THE STRODE PUBLISHERS

Table of Contents

THE STRODE PUBLISHERS
STRODE SUPER STAR SERIES

FULL-TIME PLAYER

BEST BASKETBALL BOOSTER

LITTLE LEAGUE LEADER

DEDICATED
TO
DAVID

WHO
MADE
THE
ALL-CITY
TEAM
AT
THE
AGE
OF
NINE

Not Welcome

When the Daleys first decided to move to the Kentucky mountains, Mr. Daley unfolded a map. "Here," he said, pointing to a dot on the map, "is the little town of Banks." Then Mr. Daley addressed his son. "That's where you'll go to school, Paul. Some call it the home of mountain basketball."

So here they were in the mountains at last. As their car strained to pull a house trailer up a narrow valley, Paul Daley observed with interest from the front seat beside his father. In the back seat his mother and two little sisters slept.

Paul's father worked for a construction company that tried to improve mountain land after it had been torn open by strip mining. Paul thought of the strip mining he had seen already in these mountains. Big machines were turning the beautiful green land into useless, barren wasteland. Included in his father's work in eastern Kentucky would be a recreation area and a lake.

The only thing that had kept the move from seeming so terrible for Paul was that his friend Ralph Saylor and his family would be moving, too. The Saylor's were supposed to arrive later in the afternoon.

The road ran beside a valley stream that rippled clear, then green, over moss-covered rocks. Trees and shrubs were colored red, yellow, orange, purple, and brown. A cabin up ahead puffed a steady little stream of smoke through its chimney top. It was beautiful country to be entering.

Spanning the stream from the road to the cabin was a high swinging bridge made of many planks and poles and wires, all helping each other to stay above water. The bridge waved gently back and forth in the mountain breeze. Upstream the wheel of a watermill turned slowly with the current of the water. A high, wooden water trough loomed across the road ahead. It carried a stream of water from a mountainside waterfall to the top of the mill wheel.

What really awakened Paul from his daydreaming was a big rough sign painted in smeared white letters on the side of the mill. Its words left no doubt about the nature of its warning: PRIVATE PROPERTY. DON'T GET NEAR THAT WATER TROUGH ABOVE. I MEAN IT. Then in sprawled, slanted writing it was signed: WIDOW STAMPS.

A figure showed itself on the shaded cabin porch. It was a woman. She looked small and frail and her face was almost covered by a huge shawl, but the corncob pipe she held in her mouth was not small, nor was it belching smoke in a small way. A long shiny rifle dangling from her hands reflected the fall sunlight in a chilling, unfriendly way.

"Dad," Paul said hurriedly to his father beside him, "do you see what I see? That woman's got a rifle. And that sign on that mill—she must be Widow Stamps. And there—look!" Paul quickly pointed. Just ahead, high over the road, but straight in the path of the top of their trailer, was the water trough. It was squarely in their path as it brought water from the waterfall across the road to the mill. Large glistening water drops now and then slid off the bottom.

"Well, I'll be," said Paul's father, abruptly halting the car. He had been so interested in both the woman and the sign he barely stopped the car before the trailer rammed the trough. Mr. Daley brushed a hand across his forehead. "Whew-ee," he exclaimed. "That little old woman over there with the rifle might just have started using it if we had knocked her trough down." He got out of the car and walked around the front to the other side. There he could look across the stream to the woman's cabin.

It occurred to Paul that the woman might not shoot near a young boy. So to help protect his father he opened his door and stepped onto the ground not far from his father. Mr. Daley muttered under his breath. "Son, tell your mother and the girls to keep inside the car."

"All right," Paul said and ducked back into the car just long enough to deliver the message to his mother. His sisters were still asleep.

"Ma'am," Mr. Daley yelled across the creek. "I'm sure that sign on your mill can't refer to us, can it? I'm here to start a conservation program up at the wide end of your valley. That property up there belongs to the state now. We need to get up before dark. So I'd be obliged if—"

Paul's father did not finish his words. Instead he and Paul both ducked and ducked quickly as a small pumpkin—of all things—came flying across the creek. It hit their car loudly on the front fender. Soggy, yellow pumpkin splattered against the black paint of the car and onto the road.

Paul was almost sure the pumpkin came from a clump of trees behind the woman's cabin. There a metal hoop that resembled a barrel hoop was nailed to a large board high up on a tree. Barely hanging around the hoop was an old piece of torn burlap sack. Paul could see the sack moving, as if a basketball or some kind of object—perhaps even a pumpkin— had just gone through the hoop.

But he could not see anyone, and the only noise he heard was from the little woman herself. Her voice—first her loud cackling laugh and then her words—was clear and loud enough for two voices to be coming from across the stream.

"In case you're wondering about me, I'm Widow Stamps and nobody else, and you aren't telling me nothing about who that land belongs to up there. As for that sign, it's my sign and you read it right to start with. No strangers—and I mean no strangers—are fooling with that water trough."

The voice of Paul's father showed increasing annoyance as he answered. "I'm here on official business, as I explained. This is a public road. And that land up there belongs to the state."

The Widow laughed again. "Well—that water trough belongs to me. All the way from that waterfall over there, which is mine, to the watermill here, which is mine. And, if need be, I can lower it so nothing gets through smaller than a June bug, I might say."

"It wouldn't stand up in court, Widow. You can't stop traffic on a public road."

The Widow laughed. "Whoo-ee. The way some people talk." She took some puffs on her pipe, smoke fiercely curling up around her head. "I'd say I'd already stopped traffic, wouldn't you, sir?"

Paul had been waiting for a chance to say something. "You're not going to let her get by with it, are you, dad? When we've come over three hundred miles. I wouldn't—I sure wouldn't."

Paul's father reached down and patted Paul's light blond hair. Paul could tell that his father was nervous. When his father called across the stream again, he did not seem as sure as he had before. "What would you do if I lifted the water trough just enough to get our trailer under it?" his father demanded.

The Widow held her pipe in her hand as she listened to this question. "That's been tried, too, mister, and it didn't work. For one thing, that trough's too heavy for just ordinary folks like you to lift. For another thing—" The Widow suddenly paused to laugh loudly again. "Those pumpkins keep gettin' harder instead of softer as each one comes across. Before long it's like getting hit by cannonballs." As if to make her point clearer, the Widow stuck her pipe back into her mouth and jerked up her long rifle. Paul thought the rifle looked as big as the porch post.

With a helpless shrug Paul's father looked at his son.

"I don't know what to do. I think she's got someone backing her up over there behind her house. Even if she wouldn't use her gun, that person might. At least he throws pumpkin like I would a marble. And besides, she's maybe related to half the people in these mountains. How am I going to hire people to help the conservation project if I make an enemy out of our only neighbor in the hollow?"

"Can't we get the police?" Paul asked. "That's what our principal did to get a fence moved away."

"I know. But if the people around here have honored the water trough this long, it'll probably take a court order to get it condemned and that could take weeks."

"Then why don't we just get out and walk on there?" asked Paul, "and leave the trailer here? Maybe, that way—well, who knows—"

"I'm sorry, son," his father interrupted. "We'll need the trailer to live in, as well as for an office." His father called to the Widow again. "All right, you win this first round, but I'll promise you one thing. Even though we back our trailer down the hollow this time, the upper end of your valley's going to get fixed, no matter what." He muttered under his breath aside to Paul, "All right, son. Let's go."

As they turned toward the car, the Widow gave out with more laughter. It was strange laughter that seemed to echo in all directions at the same time—up and down as well as back and forth across the hollow and across the mountains on each side. Quite clearly the Widow did not seem to think they would ever build anything on that mountain.

Just as his father was starting the engine, Paul glanced out the window on his side. What caught his attention was a large man dressed in overalls appearing from behind the Widow's cabin. The man carried a big round bundle of rags that had been tied up in a ball-shape. Then the man lifted the bundle in his powerful arms and shot it toward the basket. It went through the hoop, causing the burlap sack once more to jerk back and forth. As soon as he had made the shot, the large man disappeared again behind the house.

"I caught a glimpse of the man who must have thrown that pumpkin, dad. A big man. He's playing basketball with a ball made out of rags."

His father also looked, but the man already was gone.

"I sure hope all the basketball players around here aren't like that," said Paul and tried to laugh.

His father laughed weakly, also. "I told you I'd get you here in time for the basketball season, Paul. But I didn't know we'd get pumpkins thrown at us, to say nothing of flashing rifles and—" His father interrupted himself to start backing the trailer slowly down the road.

"Neither did I," Paul agreed, and his sober eyes began looking toward a side mirror in case his dad needed help.

But in a moment both father and son gave a last look toward the widow. For some reason she had put down her rifle and corncob pipe, and now was only pointing her walking cane. She seemed to realize that she had won her argument.

Guiding a house trailer backwards a mile down the steep, winding valley was difficult. Sometimes Paul had to get out and give his dad directions around sharp curves. Yard by yard they backed down toward the town of Banks in the valley. The only really startling

She seemed to realize that she had won her argument.

event came about a half mile down when a large snake slid down the nearby mountainside and glided near their front bumper and on across for a drink in the stream. "Wow," said Paul. "I'm glad I was in the car when he went by!"

After what seemed like a terribly long time, the

trailer neared the bottom of the hollow. In a cleared place among some trees Paul's father turned the trailer around.

As they headed toward town, it was easy to see where Banks got its name. It lay on both banks of the stream that came from the Widow Stamps' valley. Paul's father parked their trailer along a curb not far from a service station.

"Now," said Paul's mother, "that we've got this trailer down the valley, someone tell me what this is all about." As she spoke, Paul's two younger sisters, Kay and Geraldine, woke up. His mother put a calming hand on each of their heads.

Paul understood the annoyance in his dad's voice. "A widow named Stamps evidently thinks she owns the whole state of Kentucky."

"But how did she stop you?" demanded Paul's mother. "I didn't want to stare outside our car."

"She had a rifle, mother," answered Paul. "That's all dad needed. That and somebody throwing pumpkins our way, when he wasn't practicing basketball."

"Now wait a minute," said Paul's father hurriedly and gave a quick laugh. "There's nothing to be that scared about. She didn't actually point the rifle at us. And though someone did hit the side of the car with a small pumpkin, we didn't actually see anyone throw it."

"Well, it didn't just rain down on us," objected Paul.

"Sh-h," his mother cautioned, quite clearly more interested in Mr. Daley's remarks than Paul's. "Well, John, what do you plan to do now?" she asked her husband.

"I'm going to let Mr. Randolph make the decision. That's why he's the boss. I'll go to that station and phone him."

"Good," said Paul, glancing toward a cold water fountain near the station building. "That will give me a chance to get a drink of cold mountain water. Maybe that at least will be good!"

"Then I'll clean up Kay and Geraldine," said Paul's mother. She glanced about the sleepy town with its many shady trees nearby. "I surely hope—I surely hope we don't have to camp in the middle of Banks."

"We won't be camping here," her husband assured her. "We'll work it out some way. I promise."

As father and son headed across the street—the father toward a phone booth and the son toward a water fountain—Mrs. Daley and the girls went inside the trailer. Banks might be the home of mountain basketball as Mr. Daley had said, but so far it was a home without any fun.

Basketball Country

Paul's father finished his phone call and Paul his drink of water at the service station.

"I told Mr. Randolph what happened," Paul's father said, "and he said he'd call me back within an hour. So all we can do is wait until he decides what to do."

After they talked this over with his mother, Paul said, "I think I'll walk a little. That could be the school up there resting against the side of the mountain. I'd like to find out about their basketball gym."

"It's a good idea, Paul," agreed his mother. Her smile showed that she too was ready to try and make the best of a bad situation. "Just be sure you're back in an hour. And while you're doing that, the girls and I can walk around and see what stores they have in town."

"Bye," said Paul, "I'll remember. Back in an hour."

He was already on his way. He walked along a sidewalk a short distance, then saw a path through some woods between him and the school. Though Banks students probably came this way to school, only trees and a creek and a footbridge greeted him now. At last he arrived where the path ended up on the mountainside near two large brick buildings. Inscribed over the door of one building were the words BANKS ELEMENTARY SCHOOL. Over the door of the other building was BANKS HIGH SCHOOL. Alone in the school parking lot was one old car. He remembered that this was Saturday and no school was being held and wondered who was at the school.

Though Banks students probably came this way to school, only trees and a creek and a footbridge greeted him now.

Between the buildings there was a long stone foundation and many dark ashes. Somehow something suggested to Paul that those dark ashes did not spell good news for him. He hurried to the elementary school.

The front door was not locked. After hesitating only briefly, Paul slipped inside. The floors were polished and shining just the same as at his former school. But it was not until he opened the door which he hoped led to the gym that he found the owner of the car. And instead of entering a gym he found himself in a small auditorium where a man was arranging chairs on the stage. The man must have heard the door open because—though he continued working—he was looking at Paul.

"Sir," Paul called, "I wanted to see what the school gym looks like if it's all right."

"It'd be all right, son, if we had one. But we don't. The ashes out there next to this school building are all we got now. Sorry, but it burned to the ground a month ago. All the place the boys have left is a feedstore downtown."

Paul caught his breath. "What!" he called.

But the man, having said what he had, already was busy again with his work.

Paul refused at first to believe what he had heard. No gym here at Banks. It just could not be. The school principal had told his father long distance over the phone that Banks had a good basketball program. There was not any way to have a good basketball team with the school gym burned to the ground!

Paul left the school but then stopped to stare at an old home. It looked as bad off as the basketball program here at Banks, he decided, before continuing on.

It looked as bad off as the basketball program here at Banks.

Though Paul was only nine years old, he enjoyed a number of sports. He had played his first year of basketball when he was seven and thoroughly liked the game. But now he had learned that Banks did not even have a gym. What would school be like without basketball? He was asking himself this question when he happened to remember the man's last words, "the feedstore downtown."

Paul took the shortcut back through the woods, and

then he searched ahead for a building that could be the feedstore. For the first time he saw how pretty the town was down here. He had been too involved with his own thoughts to notice before. Trees lined the streets of neat houses down on this side of the woods. Over the trees a tall church rose toward the sky. He began to walk faster. Maybe the feedstore was not so bad. Maybe there was a good gymnasium after all.

Paul asked a passerby the directions to the feedstore, "where maybe they're playing some ball." The man gave Paul a curious look but then pointed toward a long brick building. "Go on back behind that general store. There's a loading platform leading to an old feedstore there in back."

Paul tried to guess from the man's tone whether or not he thought much of it as a place for playing basketball. Paul could not, but after he walked back around the corner of the building and climbed up onto the concrete loading platform and looked inside he saw too readily for himself. Though the former feedstore was big enough for a gym and though there were any number of boys inside playing basketball, the lighting was so poor Paul could not really tell how many boys were there. Only three dim lights shone overhead, and there were absolutely no windows. Paul had to let his eyes adjust to the dimness. The only person inside who was not playing ball was a thin older man who leaned against an unheated stove on this side of the court.

Paul went toward the man. He could see now that there were practice games at both ends of the basketball gym—if he could call it that. The older boys were at one end and younger boys at the other. In each group the boys were divided by those with shirts on and those who wore no shirts. Only a few wore basketball shoes while others played in their socks or bare feet. Instead of the smooth floor expected on a real basketball court, the floor was made of rough wood as Paul had once seen in a country store. Paul thought that these boys must really have tough feet and wondered if their basketball playing was just as tough.

"This isn't a regular school game, is it, mister?" Paul addressed the elderly man and hoped very much that the man would say it was not.

"Nope. Just a bunch of boys with a lot of energy on a Saturday afternoon, I reckon. And no place else to play, since the regular gym burned down."

"I see," Paul said. "Are you the coach, sir? I was hoping maybe you might be." As soon as he spoke, Paul realized that he was not exactly telling the truth. He had only wondered if the man might be the coach. So Paul corrected himself. "I meant—you're the only grown up here."

The man laughed. "The coach? That's a good one. No. I just work here. Keeping this place clean—which I'm supposed to be doing now." He laughed again. "No offense, son, I just found it funny, is all. Me—the coach? But I do know this. Basketball tryouts are after school Monday. If you want to go out there and practice now, I did hear them say they needed a practice player today." The man nodded toward the game of younger boys at the right end of the court.

"I sure would like to," Paul agreed, "but I've got to get back in an hour. The clock at the station said almost two when I left. You wouldn't happen to—"

"Sure enough," interrupted the man and pulled out a watch on a chain. "Looks by this like you got a half hour." As soon as the man returned the watch to his pocket, he put two fingers in his mouth and made a loud whistle. "Hey! Hey! You boys out there use another player?" he called.

It was not clear whether or not anyone out there heard him. But one thing was clear to Paul. No one acted as if he did. They just kept on playing.

"That makes no never mind," said the man. "Just head out. Somebody will probably let you in."

"Well, I don't know. If they heard you, they don't seem to want anybody." But even as Paul spoke he knew that—welcome or not—he wanted very much to go out. He had to have some good news about this basketball thing at Banks. So far it had been almost altogether bad. He had to find out if it was easier to play out there on that shadowy court, on that uneven floor, than it looked here from the sidelines. Almost before he realized it he was heading toward the scrimmaging players at the right end of the court.

He was barely to the group when someone yelled toward him. "Leave your shirt on. You're a shirt player." The boy who yelled this wore nothing from his waist up. The way the boy sounded, Paul figured, either he was angry because the shirt side was getting another player, or he thought that Paul should have known without being told that he would be on the side with the shirts on.

Paul had barely answered, "Good," when somehow, before he expected it, a player threw him a hard pass. It was before his hands expected it, too. With a great amount of effort Paul captured the ball.

As soon as Paul realized that he had control of the ball, he saw something else—a large opposing player bearing down on him, a boy with big muscles flexing across his bare chest and arms. He wore a defiant expression on his face.

But just as Paul saw this, he also saw a shirted player open, and Paul flipped him the ball with a quick bounce pass. It was the best play Paul had, but another player saw it in a different light. "That stranger must have seen you get him in your sights, Billy C.," the player called to the big boy. "I don't reckon I ever saw a boy get rid of a ball that fast before."

Amid the laughter that followed, Paul's face felt warm as he glanced at the player who had made the remark. The boy was about as tall as the player called Billy C., but quite a bit slimmer.

One player interrupted his laughter enough to call out, "You tell 'em, Ken!"

Paul tried to keep his mind on the game instead of the words. It did not seem to help any to reason that the boys called Billy C. and Ken had acted like this because he was a newcomer. A stranger here in these mountains, where everyone knew each other so well, might be even less welcome than anyplace else. What hurt was, absolutely the only thing he had looked forward to at Banks was playing basketball in a place that was supposed to be basketball country. He started to feel sorry for himself and so decided instead to think only of this particular game at this particular time.

If he got into the clear, maybe he would get another pass. But even this did not help. As it turned out, that opening pass to him must have been an accident. Or maybe someone had thrown him a hard pass thinking he might drop it in surprise. Because one thing now—if nothing else—grew clear. None of the players, either

shirted or shirtless, seemed to want to pass. All they
wanted was to shoot as soon as they got their hands on
the ball. They barely dribbled at all. True, as the
minutes passed—without Paul getting his hands again on

*All they wanted was to shoot as soon as they got their
hands on the ball.*

the ball—a number of the boys proved themselves to be surprisingly good shots. But Paul knew this was no way to win ball games—alone. You had to do more than shoot. You had to pass and dribble. Surely everyone knew that!

Suddenly Paul saw a chance to get his hands on the ball again. The ball was rebounding off the backboard, and though all the players were going for it Paul saw a chance to reach over someone's shoulder, bat it into the air, and grab it. This he did, spreading his legs apart as he jumped into the air, as his coach last year had taught him, so that his legs could help somewhat in keeping people off him. Landing with the ball he found himself alone. But again this was not for long. The big boy named Billy C. seemed to think this newcomer was his own special bait. It could have been Paul's imagination, but it even seemed that the other players waited a little to give Billy C. more room to speed toward him.

Except that this time Paul did not do as before. He did not get rid of the ball so fast. This time no one could accuse him of having been hurried by a boy named Billy C. Instead Paul faked as if to shoot, in order to bring the other boy's feet up off the floor. This the fake did. Then Paul broke into a fast dribble around Billy C., and it was a great idea except for one thing. This one thing maybe explained why other players were dribbling so little and shooting so much. The floor was too rough for real, fast dribbling. Paul had barely taken two steps when the ball took a crazy bounce and spun away to one side. With a silly hand-wave Paul tried to grab it, but too late. It reached someone else's hands, and that someone else of course turned with the ball and shot.

There were laughs from some of the players. Paul wondered if he himself would have found it funny if a newcomer joined a game and missed a dribble like that. As he thought about this, Paul decided he wanted to drop out of the game and wished he had never gotten in it to start with. But dropping out, of course, would not do. That would not be a way to come to Banks. The others might think he was yellow, or just a plain quitter on his first day in town. No. He should keep on trying.

Buildings In The Sky

Luckily, Paul's desire to be rid of the feedstore game was answered from an unexpected source. To Paul's pleasure he heard a familiar voice calling from within the back doorway. "Paul, the phone call came early. We've got to hurry. Come on."

Paul was embarrassed at his father having to look him up, yet he was pleased to be called away so it would not look like he quit because the game was too hard. "Bye," he forced himself to call back as he hurried away. But he could not really put much feeling into his polite farewell. They had not been polite to him.

"What's wrong?" his father asked him. "Those boys were pretty tough basketball players, eh?"

Paul agreed with a nod.

"The whole season's ahead of you, son. You can't do

it all the first day."

His father's calmness rubbed off on him, as it so often did, and Paul turned now and looked up at him. "I hadn't thought of it that way, dad. As you say, this is just the first day. Anyway—" They were on the street now, and Paul glanced in the general direction of their house trailer some distance away. "What did Mr. Randolph say to do? You know—I mean about Widow Stamps at the mill?"

At this his father suddenly grinned. "You'll never believe it, Paul, how we're going to beat that little rap. Want to hear?"

Paul nodded a quick yes.

"Well, if I told you our trailer will be flying over the Widow's cabin by helicopter some time today, what would you think of that? And not only that, the trailer of your friend, Ralph Saylor, will be carried over by another helicopter. That way the Saylors won't have to confront the Widow's water trough either. To say nothing of backing down a mile-long hollow."

Amazed at the idea, Paul halted and stared up at his father.

Mr. Daley patted him on the shoulder. "Let's go. We don't have time to stand and talk. The Saylors are already here and waiting with mother. Two helicopters are on their way."

"But why, dad? ' mean, how?" Paul hurried to catch up.

"Well, it's the smartest plan in the world, when you stop to think about it. Mr. Randolph just happened to remember that they've been using helicopters to move heavy equipment as well as huge trees. And he says the helicopters can pick up house trailers without even knowing they're doing it." His father's grin increased. "Now don't you think that's a smart way to meet a little problem on the ground. Just fly over it in the air?"

"You mean his helicopters really can lift house trailers and everything?" Paul asked.

His father laughed beside him. "We sure will see."

What they saw, and what in particular people on the ground saw later, were two trailers rising upward across a dark blue sky late on a Kentucky afternoon. One of the first to make something of this sight was a gas station attendant at the station visited earlier by Paul and his father. The attendant was putting gas in a customer's tank when he happened to see what he first thought was the roof of his station gradually rising into the air. Then he saw that, instead, it was an entire house trailer from somewhere rising gently up and over the town of Banks. The gas attendant's hands became so nervous he started hitting the hose's metal nozzle against the inside of the gas tank. Then suddenly, after he more or less had become used to one large object flying overhead, here came another hard on the heels of that one. The attendant became so excited now he stood straight up and stared toward the sky, his gas nozzle suddenly dry.

The boy they had called Billy C. at the basketball game saw that same strange sight, also. On his way home from the feedstore he headed up a small hollow that went off to one side near the lower end of the Widow Stamps' valley. He was crossing a small footbridge over a branch. First he heard the helicopter's roar, and after this he looked up to see a trailer moving overhead maybe a thousand feet in the air.

Billy C. was such a strong young athlete with a good

The attendant became so excited he stood straight up and stared toward the sky, his gas nozzle suddenly dry.

sense of balance he did not fall off the small footlog at once. As it was, he simply began weaving back and forth as he looked upward. It was not until the second trailer came into view overhead that Billy C. actually fell. He slid off feet first into the branch, as water splashed up over him.

Billy C. climbed up out of the branch and continued on into the yard of an old frame house that took up quite a bit of space on a cleared area of land. Several children in the yard, all of them younger than Billy C., stared at his dripping figure but none laughed. Even the chickens roaming aimlessly around the yard were not cackling. Nor was the hog that was rooting under the edge of the slanted front porch grunting with pleasure. Everything in the yard looked almost as defiant as Billy C.

Up on the porch it was different, though. The porch was actually a wide wooden sidewalk under a roof that went around the long frame building on all four sides. On one area of this never-ending porch sat four men, one of them older, two of them middle-aged, and one younger. They were all leaning back in cane-bottom chairs. Two of them had cups in their hands, and one had a glass and one a jug. They were drinking. Or that is, they were drinking at first. Then suddenly the buildings passed overhead and got far enough along the sky so that without moving their chairs the men could see above the edge of the porch roof. Then the four drunk men started looking at what they were drinking and then at each other and then at the sky and again at each other. Neither one let on to the other that he had seen anything.

Billy C.'s last name was Stamps. He and all his kinfolk in that big house in Bear Branch Hollow were relatives of Widow Stamps. And on this late Saturday afternoon their relative the Widow was feeling better than usual. She had done a good day's work. She had protected her property in the narrow valley. It reminded her how she had grown to womanhood when people desiring law enforcement saw about it themselves. She had grown to be an old woman without her idea of law changing. If you needed to protect your property rights, you had to do it yourself. Yes. No one would do it for you. There were other reasons, too, why she did not want the water trough above the road moved. But for today it was enough to say that it meant for Widow Stamps the protection of her property.

Because the Widow felt so good, she was even blowing rings of smoke in the general direction of the distant mountain ridges. Or she was until something started affecting her ancient eyes, and she began blinking. Could it be this dad-ratted tobacco she was smoking? She removed her pipe, stopped her rocker, and with her free hand reached automatically for her rifle leaning back against the porch wall. "Zeke, boy," she called. "See you a second, please?"

From around the corner of the building, still carrying his cloth basketball, came the Widow's boarder—the large man Paul had seen earlier. Dressed only in overalls and old shoes, he did not look much different than some of the men down on Billy C.'s porch, except that in Zeke's case he had just one eye. He squinted his good eye toward the Widow and nodded.

The Widow continued looking up. She attempted to figure out what she might or might not be seeing in a sky that could be far or near.

"Your Widow's having trouble with her poor old eyes lately, Zeke. I reckon that's just two birds out there—big ones I might add—isn't it? Looks like they're somewhat between us and that distant mountaintop and coming this-a-way."

Zeke looked toward where the Widow was looking, and slowly his mouth dropped open. His vision through one eye was no better than the old woman's because he shook his head and held up two fingers, then three, then four.

What was confusing Zeke as well as the Widow was the slanting rays of the afternoon sunlight, hitting first one metal object in the sky and then another, making them even harder to see.

Then suddenly the Widow rose from her rocker, returned her pipe to her mouth, and leaned forward on her rifle for support. The objects were getting near enough for her to see. "Well, I'll be dad-rat!" she exclaimed, "I thought I'd seen everything in these eighty-two years. Except lowered taxes and buildings flying 'round. And now I've seen everything 'cept lowered taxes."

Zeke was still staring open-mouthed.

The Widow looked toward the large sign printed in smeared letters on the millhouse. "Just what would you do, Zeke, if somebody kept you from going up a road?" She turned to him with a twinkle in her eyes. "You'd fly, wouldn't you? Of course that'd be the first thing you'd think of. You'd just fly over it."

Zeke nodded.

"Come now," the Widow said, her tone a little sharper. "Brighten up, boy. One of those things up there was down here today. You remember that car pulling that house trailer you played a little basketball with while ago? That's the trailer up there."

His vision in his one eye seemed to improve because he closed his mouth entirely before nodding again.

"Those blades turning above 'em, I reckon they're whirlybirds. They're like airplanes that can't decide whether to go up or sit down."

Zeke reached forward and put his hands on the Widow's rifle.

But she shook her head. "No, Zeke. It's no law broken if you fly through the air. You couldn't hit 'em anyway from here on the ground." She looked at Zeke and grinned. "Like I told you about basketball, boy. You can miss the first basket and still be winning a very good game."

They stared upward again and turned their heads as the two helicopters and two house trailers sailed on overhead. Then the Widow sat back in her rocker, laid the rifle across her lap, and with her other hand made her pipe more comfortable in her mouth. But she was not rocking nearly as calmly as she had been doing minutes before.

At last Widow Stamps removed her pipe just enough to say, "That's pretty smart doings, flying over that trough after all, I reckon. I'll give 'em that. That much they earned. But they can't head on up this hollow and fix 'em a pretty place without trucks going in and out some day. Eh, Zeke?"

Zeke agreed, and then vaguely nodded at his large cloth ball. He began tossing the ball up and catching it again as if anxious to get back to his one-man basketball game.

The Widow continued rocking and smoking. "And when that day comes they'll be back at the Widow's water trough. And then we'll catch 'em in our net, eh, Zeke?" Widow Stamps laughed in her loud, shrill voice. "Yes," she repeated. "Then we'll catch 'em in our net."

The Chase

While people on earth spilled their gasoline, lost their balance, or stopped their rocking, Paul was having an excellent time overhead. Riding in one of the helicopters he found Widow Stamps' valley even more beautiful from the air than it had been from the car.

Yet one thing did bother him, and it was that big torn-up area at the upper end of the Stamps' narrow valley. Somehow, it reminded Paul of mud on the big end of a spoon, with the Widow's narrow valley being the spoon handle under it. Strip mining had gouged deep holes into the earth in the big muddy part of the spoon. Where coal had once rested under beautiful leaves and moss and rich soil, there were now only large muddy ditches and dirty pools of water. It looked like a bad disease had killed every bit of life on it.

Paul's father and his mother and sisters and the Saylor family had gone up in their cars to the wide, muddy end of Widow Stamps' valley. Now they stood at the edge of the forest and motioned for the helicopters to lower the two house trailers just barely inside the forest this side of the wide, muddy area.

It was a nice peaceful spot beside the same stream that came off a distant mountain, down across the muddy area, and then down into the narrow, winding valley and on past the mill. The two families waved goodbye to the helicopters and then began to settle in as twilight and then nightfall came. On each side of the

It was a nice peaceful spot beside the stream that came off a distant mountain.

road in the forest below the trailers, the muffled night sounds of frogs and birds and water falling over rocks lulled the families to sleep.

Paul's mother had heard that some of the church people here in the mountains handled rattlesnakes during their church service or so she explained the next morning, which was Sunday. She had heard it during yesterday's window-shopping tour of Banks. But since she had not learned which church handled what, Paul's mother easily talked everyone into worshipping here at the head of Widow Stamps' valley this time, instead of in Banks.

Then on Sunday afternoon Paul and his friend, Ralph Saylor, found themselves with time on their hands and basketball on their minds. Paul's tousled blond hair perhaps suggested an athlete's, and Ralph's neatly-combed black hair and thick glasses may have suggested a student. But Paul knew how much Ralph liked basketball, too. In fact, Ralph had gone out for the same basketball team last year when Paul played first string.

"Wait till you see their gym, Ralph," Paul was telling his companion as they tossed rocks toward the stream. "That feedstore I told you about is almost like playing in a cave."

"That would make it pretty dark," Ralph agreed.

"It is. I would almost rather be playing behind that Widow's house, where the man was shooting with pumpkins and clothes and everything else."

"And throwing a pumpkin at your car," Ralph added, remembering all the exciting conversation they had last night about what had happened in the area of the Widow Stamps cabin. "What is that water mill for anyway?" Ralph asked.

"Dad says it is a grist mill. The water turns the wheel to make the power to turn two giant stones together. You put the corn between the stones, and it is ground into meal."

"I remember reading about that," Ralph said. "I think the early Greeks used water power that way, too."

Paul, who seemed to be thinking of something else now, halted in the middle of picking up a rock and, instead of throwing it, exclaimed, "I've got it! Let's fix our own basketball court. When we were driving into the mountains here, almost every house we saw had a board and hoop nailed to a tree. I've brought my ball and hoop along. I wish dad had let me bring the backboard, too."

"I'm sure there wasn't room," Ralph said. He began looking down through the forests, squinting through his glasses. "I don't know what we could use," he said and shrugged.

"Oh, I know," said Paul and looked down the valley toward the Widow's cabin, that was hidden from sight but less than a mile below. "There was a wooden sidewalk on the other side of the stream going down to the Widow's cabin. And near that sidewalk was a pile of old boards."

"After what you said about her, she doesn't seem like the kind of person who would let you have the boards," Ralph said.

"But maybe she's cooled down. And anyway, it seemed like mainly her water trough she didn't want bothered." Paul looked toward a huge oak tree not far from the trailers just down inside the forests. It would make an ideal place for putting up a board and a goal.

And if he had learned anything at all at the feedstore yesterday, it was the importance here of being a good basketball shot. Yes, he had almost an overpowering urge to get busy right now practicing basketball.

Paul turned again to Ralph. "Let's try it." When Ralph hesitated, Paul said, "We can be there and back before our parents know we're even gone." Ordinarily Paul would suggest asking their parents' permission. But knowing what they felt about the Widow, he decided not to chance it now. Basketball was simply too important to risk their parents saying no.

During their trip to the Widow's, however, Paul and Ralph had plenty of opportunity to wish that someone had said no. It was an afternoon they would never forget, although it started calmly enough. It started calmly as they trotted side-by-side down the road toward the Widow's, seeing nothing unusual at first except an old pickup truck parked off the road under a tree that shaded a gentle curve in the stream. Then as they passed they saw a young man holding a long-handled pole, with a minnow net on the end out over the stream. He was dressed in jeans, and his muscular arms were much in evidence under the short sleeves of a white sport shirt. He gave the boys a friendly enough nod as they trotted past, and they nodded quickly in return. It somehow made them feel better to have someone nod to them as they neared the Widow's. But since their main concern remained ahead, they soon forgot the muscular fisherman and hurried on their way to see what they could get done.

As they passed the millhouse, they thought they heard some noises inside. Or it could just have been the noises of the water hitting the many posts that held up the millhouse out in the stream. They ran on past, their main interest now toward the cabin, and Paul said aside to his companion, "Let's cross the bridge and go on over. Maybe, anyway, that'll be fun."

"I hope so," said Ralph with an uncertain glance toward the cabin.

Paul led the way onto the bridge and started across, with Ralph close behind. They were about to the middle of the bridge when suddenly Paul, and then Ralph, slowed. The reason was a figure that seemed to have raced out of the millhouse onto the wooden sidewalk at the opposite bank and was now gaining speed and getting close to the bridge. Suddenly Paul recognized the approaching, racing figure as the same big man who had appeared from behind the Widow's cabin yesterday. Except that right now he was neither holding a pile of clothes nor a pumpkin. Instead, upraised in his arms was an axe, blade forward as he came racing toward them. And he had one eye only—an eye that seemed set toward the boys on the bridge, who had now come to an abrupt halt.

"I'm leaving!" exclaimed Ralph and quickly began putting his words into action. But he was hard-pressed to keep ahead of Paul who was running as fast as he could without stumbling over his slower-running friend. Their rapid change of direction and new burst of speed caused the bridge to start swaying crazily under them until they felt they would surely fall into the stream. They began stumbling sideways as well as running forward, grabbing for the two hand cables that formed the sides of the bridge. By the time they neared the end of the bridge they could feel and hear the rumble of planks behind them growing rapidly closer. As Paul jumped the last of the bridge and landed on the road just behind Ralph, he glanced over his shoulder. Though the boys no longer were on the bridge, the man, instead of slowing, was coming on, seeming if anything to gain more speed. Amazingly he was keeping his balance on the swinging bridge while his hands still held the axe upraised—its sharp blade forward—instead of his hands touching the cables for support.

After another desperate glance over his shoulder, Paul cried to his running companion. "Run, run!" Paul was holding back to keep from leaving him. "He's already off the bridge and catching up!" Paul added.

True enough, instead of the rumbling bridge behind them, now came the sounds of heavy footsteps on the road. Nearby also was another sound, at about the same time they were passing the millhouse. The sound came from within the millhouse and sounded like a high cry of merry laughter. Or was it? Could it instead have been the whistling of the wind forcing its way into their mouths and ears as they ran?

Surely they would be unable to stay ahead much longer. The heavy sounds of running footsteps now were too close behind. Their lungs would almost certainly burst if they continued racing longer.

Paul and Ralph were passing the old pickup, but in their terror they did not look aside toward it or the fisherman. They just kept running as best they could, tiring as they were.

Then suddenly they heard the heavy footsteps behind them slow and then halt. It was just in time, too, and both boys, fighting for air, began slowing their pace. Paul halted entirely and looked back first. "Hey," he called out. "Ralph. Look." Ralph was breathing too

Now came the sounds of heavy footsteps on the road.

heavily to speak, but he turned enough to see back down the road.

In the middle of the road stopped dead still was the one-eyed man. His axe was dangling now beside him. The muscular fisherman was holding his pole straight across the road, barring the one-eyed man's chase after the boys. The fisherman must have swung the pole across the road just in time to let the one-eyed man know he meant business. They seemed to be arguing, too, until the fisherman looked suddenly up the road

45

and called to the boys. "Hey, you boys come back here. This man isn't going to chop you into bits, after all." There was a small hint of laughter in the fisherman's voice as he finished his words.

The two boys looked toward the two men and then toward each other.

"Maybe we'd better do as he says and go there," said Paul.

"Why?" asked Ralph.

"Well, he seems like a nice man. And the helicopters can't take us to school everyday. We have to use this road. So I think we'd better go settle it now, when maybe we've got a friend on our side."

Ralph studied his companion for a moment, then shrugged. "Well, I guess so." Then he added with a small laugh, "If we've got to get our heads chopped off, I suppose now is as good a time as any."

Startled at his companion's words, Paul stared toward him in return before breaking into a small grin also. "Yes. But if I thought there was any chance of that, I wouldn't want to go back either." The two boys began walking back down the road as requested by their new friend. At least, they hoped he was their new friend.

Up A Tree

With careful steps and eyes alert the boys neared the shadows cast by the two men on the sunny road. Then the fisherman lifted the minnow pole from in front of the axeman, turned, balanced it against the side of his truck, and faced them again. Though the man with the axe was a big man, the young man looked just as big standing beside him, and maybe even stronger.

"Zeke here was just trying to scare you boys," the young man assured Paul and Ralph who now halted cautiously several feet away. True, Paul thought, two or three yards was not much of a lead, but if the man with the axe started after them again, it just might prove the difference between life and death.

The younger man continued, "He didn't want you over to the Widow's and thought he'd scare you away.

Luckily I'd come out to have the Widow grind me some meal, then stopped here to catch me a few minnows for my grandpa's river-fishing. Right, Zeke?"

The one-eyed man nodded slowly, without words, and the boys could only hope the nod meant yes.

The fisherman smiled. Large brown freckles on his face made him appear even warmer and friendlier. "Zeke here had forgotten until I spelled it out that chasing somebody off private property is one thing. But chasing them with an axe on a public road is another. So he apologizes."

"Well, that's all right," said Ralph.

"It sure is," agreed Paul hurriedly.

"So," the fisherman continued, looking now only at Zeke. "You can run along now. And we'll all try and forget that it ever happened. OK?"

Zeke nodded slightly and then turned with a shrug and began ambling off down the road, the axe still dangling from a hairy hand.

With Zeke and his axe heading in the other direction toward the swinging bridge, and with tiny clouds of dust at Zeke's feet giving added proof that Zeke was leaving, the fisherman turned, came walking toward the boys, and extended his hand.

"I'm Cliff Barnes," he said as first Ralph and then Paul accepted his handshake. "Glad to see you boys get some color in those faces. When you passed here while ago, you were pale as my white shirt." Then he added hurriedly, as if afraid they might think he was making fun, "Not that I blame you. I'd have run, too. The thing to remember is, here in this part of the country you don't just walk up to a house unless they know you."

"You don't?" Paul exclaimed.

"That's right. Even at the Widow's, or I reckon I should say especially at the Widow's. The thing to do is stand on this side of the stream and yell across to see who's home. Then let them invite you over if they want."

"Oh I know," said Ralph, with an understanding look at Paul. "People don't like G-men who are maybe looking for moonshiners."

Paul nodded as Cliff Barnes laughed. "I'm not saying that's the reason or that it isn't. It's mainly a custom. But anyway, speaking of customs, my granddad's custom is to fish of an evening, and I've got to get these minnows home." Cliff turned as if to leave, then halted, and looked again at the boys. "Except for one thing," he said, and then looked from one to the other with his right eye partly closed, as if he himself might or might not be suspicious of them. "Just what were you boys going across the bridge for?"

"That one's easy," said Ralph without any hesitation and himself partly closing his own right eye as he looked up at the big fisherman. "We weren't hunting for a moonshine still, after all. We were looking for some boards to make a backboard to practice basketball with."

As soon as Ralph said the word "basketball," Cliff gave him a quick, serious look. "You mean you boys like basketball too?" Cliff asked and smiled. "I knew everyone in these mountains did, but I didn't expect to meet two visiting boys on the road and find them as interested as the rest of us."

"We are very interested," said Ralph. "Are you?"

Cliff grinned. "I sure am. In fact, you'd never believe it, but I even went two years to college and played,

before I had to come back here because of an
emergency at home." Suddenly Cliff interrupted himself
and stared at Paul. "Oh—I bet I get it. Aren't you the
boy who just got here yesterday afternoon and played a
little basketball at the feedstore?"

Thoroughly startled, Paul realized that Cliff was
looking straight at him. "Why yes—I guess so—I mean,
yes I am—but how—how did you know?"

Cliff chuckled. "There's very few secrets around here
is the reason. While the meal was being ground, the
Widow told me of a boy she called Cotton Top—which
means he'd have blond hair like yours—and how she
made him and his dad back their trailer down the
hollow." Cliff seemed to be grinning a little more than
necessary, in spite of himself. It was as if he had been
amused at what the Widow had told him, even though
he knew she had done wrong. Cliff added hurriedly,
"And I dropped by the feedstore later yesterday
afternoon, and they told me that a boy like you had
been there and that Billy C. had taken a dribble
away—or something." Then, even more quickly, Cliff
concluded, "And of course I doubt if a soul in these
hills missed seeing those two trailers fly over."

"Yeah," said Paul and looked at Ralph in amazement.
"I see what you mean about everybody knowing
everybody's business here."

"Especially," said Cliff, "if they arrive like you all
did. Now listen, boys. I am flat-dab, as I say, wanting to
get on home so my granddad can fish. But if there's one
thing even he wouldn't mind, it's me being late to help
with basketball doings. Especially if it concerns two
strangers that I saw going to some danger just to try and
improve their game. So I tell you—you boys come with

me. I'm not sure, but I might just have something that'll help."

"Well good," said Ralph eagerly.

"OK," Paul also agreed. Because, after all, the thing they had started all this for was yet to be accomplished. And if this man who called himself Cliff Barnes could

"Aren't you the boy who played a little basketball at the feedstore?"

help, their seemingly narrow escape with Zeke could almost be worth it.

They followed him to the back of his truck. "Here's some old lumber," he said, and held up several planks. "I've been meaning to make a bench for my granddad to use with his fishing, but there's plenty more where this came from. You see—I've even got a hammer, some nails, and a saw. How lucky can we be?"

"But we don't want to use that," said Paul. "All that's yours."

"It's mine to help you boys make your basketball backboard with. Come on now. It's not everyday I keep somebody from chasing boys with an axe, just to find out they only wanted a backboard. I'll drive you up to your trailers—it's easier to turn around up there anyway."

"Are you sure?" asked Paul.

"Listen, boys," said Cliff quickly, but his grin was still slow and friendly. "One thing about these mountains—if you'll let me spell it out. In these mountains if somebody asks to do you a favor, you'd better let them do it."

"Or their feelings will get hurt," said Ralph, who was not reluctant to let it be known that he read quite a few books. "Like visiting native tribes anywhere. If they pass the peace pipe, you're supposed to smoke it or everyone will get offended and war might break out."

Cliff laughed in amusement. "Exactly." He placed his minnow net and bucket of minnows in the back of the pickup, then opened his cab door and swung in under the wheel. Paul and Ralph promptly followed into the passenger side of the cab.

As Cliff drove them up the hollow in his pickup, he

had a feeling of satisfaction he had not known for some time. He felt responsible for saving these two boys from serious difficulty. Not that he was sure that Zeke actually would have hit them with his axe. He still tended to believe that Zeke was only trying to scare them. But one could not be exactly sure, and at the very least the powerful and bull-headed Zeke was capable of running the boys almost to death. If he did not first scare them almost to death.

And Cliff felt good for another reason. These two boys, dressed in Sunday sports clothes, were well-dressed compared to most boys in this area and so reminded him very much of his pleasant university life. The boys could have been the sons of University of Kentucky teachers or school officials that one saw so frequently on and off the campus. Yes, Cliff had enjoyed his two years in Lexington more than any two years he could remember. The basketball scholarship had been just enough to permit his wife and himself to live at the university for the two years. If only there had been no mine accident, and his father had not been killed, forcing them to return to the small farm just outside Banks to care for a mother and grandfather and grandmother.

"We sure were glad you were parked back there," Ralph was saying.

Paul nodded in agreement.

"All I did was hold out my minnow pole," Cliff said modestly, but at the same time he must agree, if only to himself, that he had done considerably more.

Paul said, "You know, I've been thinking." He glanced aside at Ralph. "If we tell our parents about the axe, they are really going to lose their cool. Especially since they didn't even know we were down there to start with."

"They sure would," Ralph added. "If I know my mother, we'd be out of Kentucky by nightfall if she heard about that axe."

"You boys just remember my advice," Cliff reminded them. "Before crossing that bridge again, get the Widow's attention, and then be sure you've got her permission before you even start across."

"You don't have to remind us of that," said Paul.

"You'd better believe it," Ralph agreed.

Cliff believed they had gotten his warning. So he, like they, did not mention the axe when they arrived at the trailer house area to be greeted by the parents of both boys. The fact that a stranger had driven up past the Widow's, and was willing to help their boys build a backboard, was interesting enough to all.

First Cliff built the backboard on the ground, straight and firm with crossboards nailed behind, the heads of the nails of course pounded down hard into the front side. Then he nailed Paul's hoop firmly onto it. Next he pulled up his truck so he could stand on it and position the backboard against the large oak until he judged the hoop to be exactly ten feet from the ground. Then he nailed the backboard against the tree. After this Paul brought his basketball from the trailer, and then the two boys and Cliff promptly tested the backboard.

Both boys missed their shots, but with surprising ease Cliff turned and spun the basketball up against the backboard and through the hoop. When the two boys complimented him, Cliff grinned. "It's easy to bank a shot off a backboard if you'll remember just to lay it there. Try not to move forward under the basket, but move up instead. Like holding up a big turkey egg, and you don't want to break its shell."

"Or a bundle of dynamite," Ralph added. "Anything you wouldn't want to break."

"Exactly." Cliff had caught his own rebound, and he held the ball for a moment while he looked from one boy to the other. "There's a lot I don't know about basketball, but sometime when I have time maybe I can point out a few things I do know—that is—of course—if you boys might think you'd want me to."

"That's great," they agreed, and at the same time Paul saw his father outside the trailer casually looking at a set of building plans in his hands. Paul turned away, then looked once again at his father. Suddenly Paul's eyes widened as an idea came to mind. "Dad, won't you be needing people to help you here?" he called.

Paul's father gave a short laugh. "That may be the understatement of the year. Somewhere I'm going to have to hire at least fifty people."

"Including somebody who is maybe real good with a hammer and nails?"

"Especially somebody who's real good with a hammer and nails."

"Well—" Paul nodded toward Cliff Barnes and then looked again at his father. "Maybe you should come over here a bit, dad. Do you mind?"

Cliff stared from Paul to his father and said nothing as Paul's father approached. Mr. Daley reached out and shook hands with Cliff. "My name's Daley," he said.

"Glad to meet you, Mr. Daley. My name's Cliff Barnes." Cliff paused a minute before asking, "Just what all are you going to do up here? We hear all kinds of rumors in town—"

"Well," Mr. Daley began, as if pleased he was asked. "You know the upper part of the valley here was laid to waste years ago because of the strip mining of coal. So today the federal government is helping the state of Kentucky reclaim this land. We're going to try to fill up all the ravines and gullys—smooth things up a bit—plant trees, build a recreation area, a dam—"

"A dam?" Cliff interrupted.

"Yes," Mr. Daley said. "We call it a prefabricated dam. We build a kind of frame for it across the stream and then we'll haul up the middle section." He paused. "I guess owing to the Widow's trough, we'll fly up the middle section." Everyone laughed. Then he continued. "We'll drop that middle section into the frame. Just like putting a window in a window frame."

"But won't that dry up the creek?" Cliff asked.

Mr. Daley explained. "No, not really. We can control the water passing through the dam. It'll drop the level of the creek pretty low at first until the lake fills up. But not so low that it will destroy the wildlife in the stream."

"But, dad," Paul interrupted, "won't that hurt the Widow's mill?"

"Well. The stream won't be strong enough to turn her wheel, that's for sure," his father replied. "But then she's got the water trough that feeds water to the top of her mill wheel."

Paul, still not satisfied, questioned his dad further. "Why are they building a lake anyway?"

"Well, son, the land here is in pretty bad shape as is evident. Also, the washes and gullys are holding polluted water. When we get these bulldozers going and fill up those holes, all that extra water is going to be running into the stream. A lake will balance things off a little more. When the lake reaches a certain level, we'll increase the flow of water through the dam into the stream. Then everything will be back to normal. OK?"

"OK, dad." It wasn't that Paul necessarily liked the Widow or even felt sorry for her. He was afraid if his dad were to do something that kept her water mill from working, everyone in the town might turn against them. And silently remembering the chase with the axeman, he was afraid that it might not take much to get these people mad.

"It sounds real good to me, Mr. Daley," Cliff said. "My granddad says years ago he used to hunt in this upper valley area before the strip mining began. It really hurt him to come up here afterwards and see it all torn up. I think what the government's doing—trying to restore this area—make it useful again—is a real good thing."

"Well then, how about it?" Mr. Daley said. "Think you'd like to work for us?"

"Please do," said Paul. "Please do."

"We promise not to bug you about basketball until after work," Ralph added.

"Well—" Cliff looked from one boy to the other and then again at Paul's father and slowly grinned. "At that, almost all my crops are in," he said. "So why not?"

Cliff pushed out a powerful hand to Paul's father, and as the two men shook hands it was clear that each liked the other and what each other had in mind.

Too Many Players

Next day Paul and Ralph walked down the valley to school—straight past the Widow's—without a sign of either her or Zeke. And after their first day of school, spent mostly in finding their way around and meeting teachers and pupils, they walked straight to another place of interest, and that was a feedstore.

When Paul and Ralph got to the feedstore, it looked as if all the children in Banks had gathered to play ball in this substitute gym. There was barely room to even change clothes. On Saturday Paul had noticed a wooden partition just inside and to the left of the door, and today he and Ralph learned its purpose. The only undressing and dressing area turned out to be a place crowded with benches on this side of the gym floor. Today they found the area crowded with boys changing clothes.

"Hey, look what we got here," said an all too-familiar voice as Paul and Ralph were tying the laces of their gym shoes. "A couple of new fancy-looking ball players." It was Ken Kerr, the tall thin boy that Paul had played with Saturday, calling from the far end of the dressing area.

Paul nudged Ralph. "Don't pay any attention," he said. "He was talking like that on Saturday too." Paul looked about the room but did not see the other player he had reason to remember—the boy named Billy C.

Suddenly from out on the ball court a heavy voice boomed. "OK, you boys ages nine, ten, and eleven still in the dressing area. It's time to get started. Get on out here."

The voice had a businesslike tone to it, and the boys apparently sensed it. They began hurrying to him from the dressing area, even before the speaker's huge arms motioned for them to hurry more. Paul noted with pleasure that only seventeen or eighteen boys were crowding at this end of the court. The other end was for the many younger boys in the feedstore.

"I'm Coach Bell," the big heavyset coach began without any loss of time whatsoever. "I want to welcome you to practice. I'm pleased that instead of regular physical education as your last class of the day, you've chosen basketball instead."

Coach Bell paused and smiled about the group. "I know some of you boys by sight. Some of you I don't. Some of you were on my team last year." The coach's smile suddenly faded. "Ken! You and Billy C. stop fidgeting. You two, of all boys, should know that when I'm talking I want everyone's attention." Paul to that moment had not noticed the boy named Billy C. being part of this group. But now, sure enough, here he was just like Saturday, except that unlike Saturday the big boy had on a practice jersey, although an old one, as well as basketball shoes.

Billy C. and Ken straightened up and started acting right, as were the other boys. It was easy to admire a coach this businesslike in these surroundings. The coach continued. "All you boys should know the problems we face this year, starting with that burned-out gym. And because of that even my assistant coach has quit, and I'm not even sure we'll get another. And of course this is not the best place in the world to practice basketball in."

There were a number of nods of agreement, accompanied by remarks such as, "You're right about that, coach. You sure are."

"But—" the coach resumed, and he straightened his large body. He had a basketball in his hands, and he slammed it down hard against the floor and caught it, as if to show the squad that he really did feel businesslike. "But," he repeated, "for quite a few seasons we've had a winning team. And this year let's try extra hard to have another. Many years ago my own coach told me that the sign of true champions is to bounce off the floor and try it again, just like I bounced that ball off the floor and caught it. No matter how hard the licks, my coach told me, a true sportsman will bounce right back! Well, over the years he's been right. That kind of attitude has made us champions on this side of the mountain for these many years. And even though we've been unable to carry our championship across the mountain and beat Marble for the championship over there, we would have won last year except for that unfortunate event, as you also know."

Here a shadow crossed Coach Bell's face as if an unpleasant picture came to mind. "Maybe I should take just a moment here to put that unfortunate event to rest once and for all. By unfortunate event of course I mean that Marble fan taking a gun and shooting the basketball out of the air just as we were about to beat Marble last year. I know that a lot of people here at Banks, including some of you boys, still hold resentment against Marble and its players and fans. And because also of other things such as pouring that bucket of water under our goal. I know it was dangerous because it resulted in injuring one of our boys when he came running down to shoot and slid into a brick wall. But that's all in the past, and my advice is for us, and everybody else in town, to try and forget it. Our job now is the future and what we can do this season. Never look back but always forward is another motto I have."

But Ken Kerr spoke up. "Except where will we play the Marble team, coach? It's our year to play the game here. But—" Ken cast his own brand of disapproving look around the feedstore. "We sure can't play it here. And as you yourself were just saying, Coach—"

"You're right," Coach Bell agreed. "Nor do any of the other teams want to play us here either. We'll have to play all our games on their courts. But we'll work something out. And anyway, that's enough of that for now." The coach clearly tried to send a smile of confidence over his squad. "You boys just remember that we can have another winning team this year, no matter what has happened in the past."

"Yes sir, yes sir!" came the response. The various

players were saying it loudly and clearly, as if they really meant it from deep inside them. Paul and Ralph found themselves joining in, although much of the coach's words had been news to them.

Everyone's actions must have been good news to Coach Bell because his smile widened. And his tone showed rising optimism too. "Basketball may look hard to learn, but if you can dribble a ball, and can pass it, and can shoot it, you have it made. Our one major fault has always been not passing enough. You boys are good shots because you practice enough at home. You have learned to jump and shoot with your right foot forward if you're right-handed and with your left foot forward if you're left-handed. You have learned at home through practice to pick out the point on the rim nearest you and aim for that. And how to guide the ball with the fingers of your left hand and push it with the fingers of your right hand when you shoot. Unless you're left-handed, when it works just the opposite. And how to roll the ball back off the tips of your fingers when you shoot. And then how to shoot the ball high in the air so that it floats down into the basket just past that point.

"But this year let's really learn how to pass, too. Remember that it's your wrist action in passing as well as in shooting that helps do the job. As for dribbling, let's not worry too much about this uneven floor. It may even have one advantage. When you dribble, you want to dribble the ball close to the floor if you can, trying to dribble it no higher than your knee." Coach Bell laughed, making the best of a bad situation. "And if you don't, on this floor you may never see the ball again. The ball may bounce all the way out the door.

OK, boys."

His enthusiasm obviously continuing, the coach slapped his basketball with both his hands. He was emphasizing his words by using his hands. "It's time now to start with the real business at hand. I want you boys to form a big circle around me, and I'll pass the ball to you and I also want you to pass it to each other.

Practice lasted two hours.

As I said—and I can't say it too much—before the season's over this year I want us to learn the pass real well."

After passing the ball, the squad formed two lines and practiced "running shots" by laying the ball softly up against the backboard. "Run as fast as you can to start with, but be sure and slow down before you get near the basket," were the coach's words. Then the squad practiced dribbling by trying to bounce the ball "no higher than the knees."

Practice lasted almost two hours before Coach Bell finally blew the whistle and said, "That's all for today, boys."

Everyone could agree that Coach Bell's team in their first practice had done well in making the best of a bad physical location.

Daniel Boone Could Shoot

After their first day of basketball practice, it was a couple of tired boys who headed up the Widow Stamps Hollow as long shadows marked approaching nightfall. Yet the boys were not so tired but what they thought of the same idea at about the same time.

"Let's start trotting," said Ralph. "It's nearing dark, and that nut is still across that bridge with his axe."

"If nothing else it will help us get in better shape," Paul agreed. As they neared the bridge, Paul whispered aside under his breath, "Let's not look like we're running from him, though. I'd even just as soon he didn't hear us pass."

But the only sign of life at the Widow's cabin was the steady stream of smoke from her chimney, smelling of burning pine and cedar. As quiet as the Widow's smoke, the boys hurried silently past and up the road toward home.

They were still only part way up the hollow when they began seeing a bright light far ahead in the shadows. They began asking themselves and each other what it was, but they did not really see until they were almost there. It was a spotlight pointed toward a tree. Suddenly they saw toward which tree and for what purpose the light pointed. It was hooked onto the cab of a pickup truck and pointed toward the basketball goal. Then out of the shadows stepped Cliff Barnes.

"I hooked this light up to a battery on the truck," Cliff greeted them, his freckle face friendly in the light. "Thought I'd take just a minute for some basketball like I promised yesterday."

"Fine," said Ralph, and "Thanks," said Paul. But neither boy felt completely overjoyed. They had seen quite a bit of basketball already today.

Cliff must have noticed the lack of enthusiasm in their tone, because he said quickly, "I know you boys are tired, and so we'll make it short. I would have gotten here earlier, but everybody in the valley can set their clock on the fact that Coach Bell lets out promptly at five. Anyway I've had other things on my mind, such as my not coming back up here, maybe."

"What!" Paul exclaimed.

"Why won't you be back?" asked Ralph.

The door of the Daley's trailer opened, and Paul's father stepped out and came walking toward the lighted area. Barely had the trailer door slammed behind him when from the Saylor's trailer Ralph's father also emerged.

"Maybe you'd better ask them," said Cliff with a nod

toward the two men as they neared the lighted area.

"Dad," Ralph greeted his father at once, "why won't Mr. Barnes be back?"

"Well, because—" Mr. Saylor hesitated and looked at Paul's father.

"Well, boys," said Paul's father. He nodded toward Cliff Barnes. "By the way, Cliff, appreciate your staying on to give them those last few minutes of instruction, as you said."

"But why, dad—what's happened?" asked Paul, now as impatient-sounding as Ralph. Being a little tired when they first got here was one thing. But the chance of not getting the promised instruction from Cliff Barnes was quite another.

"It's no big mystery," said Paul's father. "These hills, evidently, are filled with friends and relatives of Widow Stamps. And word has gotten around that the Widow doesn't want anything built here at all. So Cliff today was a one-man work force here. Of course we can't get our job done without a lot more help than just us here."

Ralph looked at Cliff Barnes. "But can't you do something about it? The way you handled things yesterday, I was hoping you could take care of anything like this."

Cliff grinned at Ralph's boyish frankness. "The two most important things around here are blood relatives and basketball," he answered. "As for blood relatives, these mountains are full of relatives of Widow Stamps. And there's probably not a one that wouldn't back her up in a showdown. As for basketball, we'd better get our quick practice in, as I promised, because I still have chores to do at home." Cliff looked at the fathers of the two boys. "If it's all right, I'd like to work with them just a few minutes to give them some ideas to practice with, as I promised them I would."

"Fine," said Paul's father, as Ralph's father nodded agreement. "We'll be back in a little, after checking some boundary lines."

"All right." Cliff turned to Paul and Ralph. "Here in this mountain league, unless you're a real good shot you're pretty well out of the running. That means guards as well as centers and forwards. Everybody practices shooting, and that's why we've got so many good shots. Of course it takes more, too, but you need to start with that." Cliff turned to a basketball lying on the ground near the front bumper of his pickup. He picked it up and tossed it to Ralph. "Give me a couple of quick points," he said. "By putting it through the hoop."

With a grin Ralph turned at once with the ball and faced the basket. He cupped the fingers of his right hand behind the ball and with the fingers of his left hand attempted to guide the ball as he shot. Ralph did exactly as he had been taught to do. He let the ball spin off the tips of his fingers as he shot. His form was correct. His grin made him look confident as he shot. The only thing was—he was about twelve feet from the basket, and the ball touched neither the basket nor the backboard. It missed completely.

Cliff scooped up the loose ball and tossed it to Paul. Paul's shot was a little better—in fact it hit the side of the basket—but as for going in, it made no more points than had Ralph's.

Ralph caught Paul's rebound, and Cliff motioned for Ralph to hold the ball.

"Boys, it isn't your form," Cliff said. "Both of you

are using the correct form—one hand behind the ball for power and the other forward to help guide it." Cliff looked earnestly from one boy to the other. "What you've got to do is aim, like old Daniel Boone used to aim his rifle in these parts. Know how that was?" Cliff looked at Ralph.

Ralph stared back, a little embarrassed. He had indeed read a large number of books, and he did not mind rattling off bits of information if someone asked him a question. But for the life of him he had never read anywhere how Daniel Boone did it when he aimed his rifle. Ralph finally had to shrug. "No. I really don't think I ever read about how Daniel Boone aimed his rifle. Not anywhere."

Cliff laughed aloud. "I'm not sure I have either. But he was a good shot, and the only way he got to be a good shot was to aim for the smallest target instead of the biggest. That way if he missed the small thing, he at least would hit the big one. Like this."

Cliff motioned for Ralph to toss him the ball. Ralph did. Cliff got set and let the ball go. It sailed high into the air and came down gently through the hoop.

"Great shot," said Ralph, nodding his head in approval.

"It sure was," Paul agreed and grabbed the ball as it came down.

"And you can do the same thing, too, if you'll aim like Daniel Boone used to and like I try to. Toward the smallest point you can imagine. If Daniel aimed toward that basket, you don't think he'd aim for all of it, do you? No. He'd pick out the smallest point on that rim, the point nearest him, and then ever so gently squeeze the trigger. In his case, if he'd been using a basketball, he'd have tossed it up just over that tiny point and let it come down on the other side. Or if he had wanted to bounce the ball off the backboard, he'd have picked a tiny point on the backboard instead."

"I get it," exclaimed Ralph. "You aim for a small point, and even if you miss that you still are pretty much on target. Here, let me try it," he said to Paul who still had the ball.

Paul hesitated, because he had gotten the ball in order that he himself could shoot. But Cliff grinned and with his head indicated Ralph, and so Paul tossed it to him. Ralph again without hesitation, though this time without his confident smile, got set and shot. His eyes were staring earnestly toward the hoop trying to pick out a small spot. It did not go in, but it was straight enough—just a little short.

"That's the idea," Cliff complimented him. "You had it in your gunsight. All you needed was a little more gunpowder. Let me show you boys what to aim at, then I've got to hurry to those chores." From the carpet of pine needles at their feet, Cliff picked up one needle. He held it up for them to look at. "See the tiny point of this needle. Now I'm going to toss the needle toward that rim and just imagine its point landing at the spot nearest you." Cliff tossed the needle toward the rim. "OK, boys," he said and began walking toward his truck. "Just imagine it's still up there. Every chance you get, just practice your shooting by looking for the nearest point on that rim. Then maybe you'll make the Banks team, unless your dads move from here first."

"It may not be much of a team, though," Ralph said. "That feedstore's something else."

Cliff swung into his truck cab, turned off his spotlight

from inside, then spoke out to the boys who now were approaching the truck. "That sure is bad about the gym," he agreed. "I don't know what this place is coming to. A gym burns down, and they say there's not enough money to rebuild it. The state wants to build a recreation area up here. And my friends and relatives around here won't cooperate."

"Even if we can't build anything here," said Paul, "I wish at least we could use that money to help the town build a gym." Ralph turned abruptly, and his large blue eyes through his glasses stared at his friend. "You just said it, Paul! You just gave the answer! You know what?" Ralph looked from Paul to Cliff Barnes, but neither indicated that they knew what he was talking about.

Ralph laughed with excitement as his idea became clearer in his mind. "I see more and more possibilities," he said, "the more I think about it. What about this?" He lowered his tone as if about to tell them a secret. "You know that our dads are hoping to build several buildings here, including a recreation building. Why not let it be used for a gym, until the town can build its own? That way the people will get behind us and—"

When Ralph finished speaking he looked first at Paul, and then both boys turned and looked up into the truck cab. It seemed clear that one person who might answer this was Cliff Barnes.

Perhaps Cliff sensed this also. Because he stared down toward the two boys, and then his face eased into a smile. "You know something," he said. He started the engine of his truck and in parting called above its noise. "That's an idea that just might win us some basketball games. Let me ask some questions of my friends, before we get in touch with your dads." He waved good-bye, put his truck in reverse, spun it around, and then went heading noisily down toward Widow Stamps Hollow.

A few mornings later as if by magic men began showing up to start work at the mountain site. The magic stayed, as the workmen began returning regularly thereafter. Of course, exciting everyone was the possibility of completing the recreation building in time to use it as a gymnasium this spring. If only it could be ready before Banks' basketball season ended. Or if not before, at least if it could just be ready for that Marble game. A favorite promise in and out of Banks became, "We'll have to finish that building at least in time to line it with marble." Painful though it might be to admit it, the Banks team and fans had in mind lining the gymnasium building with Marble players instead of the rock variety, of course.

Paul and Ralph, as pleased as they were, did not have time to ask many questions about what was happening. They were too busy at school, and after school they were busy practicing basketball at the feedstore. In the forest at home they practiced at their favorite tree.

As the basketball season progressed, they became even busier. Yet when the basketball games themselves began, there was one cloud on the horizon—as far as Paul and Ralph were concerned. Neither boy, and this included Paul, was a starter on the first team. Only when Banks pulled well ahead of given opponents, as the season progressed, would Coach Bell send in Paul at forward, and less frequently Ralph at guard. Both boys could not help but wonder if Coach Bell was so satisfied with his winning team without them, he was deciding he really did not need either of them.

In the forest at home they practiced at their favorite tree.

Even with the much-feared game with Marble getting closer and closer, Coach Bell still did not act like he really needed Paul or Ralph. Instead of thinking about Banks' players, everyone seemed to be thinking about Marbles'. "To make up for what they did to us last year," was yet another favorite expression about town. And meanwhile both boys, Paul and Ralph, wondered if they might not sit this championship out.

A Cry For Help

Then at last it came. The time for talking and for fears was past. The week of the championship game was upon them.

The Friday before the game Coach Bell called his squad together in the feedstore gym. "Well, boys, we have one more game of the season. And I don't think I have to tell you which one. Now you know that Larry Poole, first string forward, was injured in the last game. He won't be able to play Saturday against Marble." Groans came from the group, and some of the players looked at each other and shook their head, indicating that things were really not good at all.

"Remember, what I said!" Coach Bell raised his voice. "We gotta bounce back!" He slapped the ball on the floor and caught it again, then suddenly he smiled.

"And so I also have good news. Mr. Daley and Mr. Saylor called me up yesterday about the new recreation building at the upper end of Widow Stamps Hollow. As you and everybody else in town knows, they got permission to enlarge the building to gym size so we could use it until we get one built down here. Well, I had a call from Mr. Daley just a few minutes ago. The building's going to be ready for our game Saturday with Marble."

Cheers and shouts of laughter drowned out Coach Bell's voice, and he had to blow his whistle to calm the boys.

"I told you so," some of the boys began reminding each other. "I told you it'd be ready." Paul and Ralph looked at each other with surprised smiles. They, like everyone else, had known of the possibility. But even they, though living at the site, had to be told after school today that a final decision was here.

Coach Bell's booming voice resumed. "OK now! Let's get out there and play ball!"

His squad was still so excited about the news, Coach Bell repeated his instructions. But, excitement or not, the squad had its work cut out, and so began its warm-up routine as if already playing the championship game on the new home court in the Widow Stamps' valley.

"Paul Daley," Coach Bell called. "I want to see you a minute." Paul dropped out of his place in the line-up and trotted over to the coach.

"You looked real good last Saturday when I put you in after Larry got hurt. To tell you the truth I felt you could do it all along, but I was afraid the other boys might not pass you the ball." Coach Bell almost looked embarrassed as he added, "You know how hard they make it on new boys sometimes, and I couldn't risk not having everyone pulling together. Well, anyway, I've decided to let you start this Saturday against Marble." Coach Bell turned and looked at the players on the court. "In fact I think I'll let you play first-string forward." He put a hand on Paul's shoulder. "I know you can do it."

With this new happiness added to the excitement of the news about the gym, Paul was barely aware of his response. He did know that in some way he thanked the coach and made it somehow back to the lineup. And all through the rest of practice the words kept going through his head: "First-string forward, first-string forward . . ." It was why he had practiced so hard all those extra hours with Cliff Barnes, and it was finally paying off.

After practice, as Paul and Ralph walked home, Paul could still think of nothing else. This is why he did not at first realize that Ralph beside him was being so quiet. In fact, he had all but forgotten Ralph until Ralph spoke up and said, "Congratulations, Paul. You really deserved it. You really did."

Although Ralph quite clearly tried to sound sincere, something in Ralph's tone caused Paul to give him a quick look. Suddenly it came to Paul how selfish he himself was being. He asked himself what it would have felt like to be in Ralph's place. The coach had not praised Ralph. He had not put his hand on Ralph's shoulder. Yet Ralph ever since coming to Banks had been trying just as hard to play good ball as he had himself. Paul remembered how it had been in football last fall before they moved to Banks. Other players had

All through the rest of the practice the words kept going through his head: "First-string forward, first-string forward..."

called him "Little Ralph Saylor" because of his size. Yet he had tried as hard or more so than any boy on the team. Only to spend most of his time on the bench, watching the other boys have much of the fun.

"Ralph," Paul said aloud. "You're going to make it yet, in your way, you know. You're going to make it. I know you will."

Ralph hesitated, and Paul wondered at first if he might not be about to cry. But then Ralph said bravely, "Let's hope so." He turned and slapped a hand against Paul's shoulder. "The important thing is you're now solid first-string, Paul. The coach thinks you're the best."

"One day he can think that way about you, Ralph," Paul insisted. "If Mr. Cliff Barnes can help my shooting, by talking about that point on a pine needle, he can bring you around, too, Ralph. I know he will."

"It'll probably take more than that," said Ralph. "I'll never make a first team." Paul caught an uncertain sound in Ralph's voice. Neither boy said any more for a while. Besides, they were nearing the millhouse, and it was a mutual understanding that they not make noise in this area. It was not that they were exactly afraid, but on the other hand it did seem foolish to go out of their way to let Zeke know they were near.

But on this evening a sudden sound changed their desire to pass by unnoticed. The sound was a cry from within the millhouse. They heard it as they were about to go by. Both boys halted at once. Listening carefully they could distinguish amid the rushing of the water flowing through the dark underneath the millhouse the cry of a faint voice. "Help, help. Help me. Help."

Ralph and Paul stared toward the dark old stairway

leading up from the road into the millhouse, and then they faced each other uncertainly.

"It's from deep inside the millhouse," said Paul, his heart suddenly beating faster. "A voice is calling help."

"I know," Ralph agreed. "Listen."

They turned and stared toward the millhouse again. "Help. Help me," a voice called, even more clearly this time.

'We'll have to go see," said Paul, hoping that his tone sounded braver than he felt. "Someone in there may really need help."

"I know," said Ralph. "But let's be careful. It could be a trick, too, you know. I still haven't forgotten that axe. He might just be waiting inside with that axe."

Paul had already reached the stairway when Ralph said this last, but now he turned and looked back. "What kind of trick?" he whispered, his heart pounding faster again. "That voice didn't sound like Zeke's, if that's what you mean. It sounded more like a woman's—probably the Widow's."

"I know," said Ralph. "But what if they're in there together?"

"You mean—" Paul began and turned and stared uncertainly up the stairway.

"Sh-h," Ralph cautioned. "There it goes again." As both boys listened, there was the same cry for help. As soon as the plea ended, Ralph said, "Go on, please. I'm right behind you."

If Paul saw any humor in his friend's request that he go first and Ralph go second, Paul failed to show it. Instead with jaws tense and his knees feeling uncertain he began leading the way on up the steps. Surely, if someone inside the millhouse really did need help—and it was not a trick—it was not right for them to linger longer outside.

At the top, with the help of Ralph's hands reaching past Paul's wobbly knees, they pulled open the heavy, creaky door. "Where are you?" Paul called uncertainly, unable at first to see anything but shadows ahead. "Who are you? What's wrong?"

At first their only answer was a strange gurgling sound. Then a voice called from somewhere almost straight ahead near the middle of the millhouse, except that it sounded like it was under the millhouse, too. "Help me, if that's what you've come here for. Don't just stand there wiggling your toes. Before I lose my hold and slip on down and drown." It was easy to recognize the voice of the Widow now.

"All right, Widow," Paul called, leading the way as the two began moving forward toward where it sounded like the voice was from. They were afraid to move too rapidly, though, because every post at first looked like a shadowy figure. And every board that rattled under their feet seemed like it would give way under them and send them shooting down into the gurgling stream below.

"Where are you, Widow?" Paul called, surprised that his voice sounded as clear as it did in all the excitement and danger as they got deeper and deeper into the darkened building.

"I'll give you two guesses," came her reply. "I'm right here."

"But where is that, Widow?" Ralph asked.

"On down here, boys. Hurry along. I can't hold long."

As they neared her, the Widow's murmurings became

louder, helping to guide them forward.

Suddenly the Widow called up sharply from just ahead of them and below. "You boys slow it now. Watch those steps. With all three of us down in this dad-ratted hole we'll all be gone for sure."

The Widow's warning was unnecessary. They saw what she meant. A big opening had appeared suddenly in the floor, readily visible because it led straight down to the water where it captured whatever light there still was from outside.

At first they did not see the Widow. Then she called up impatiently. "Here I am. You boys open your eyes. Save your sleeping till you're home in bed." Her small hands were high above her head holding a board that went from one side of the millhouse floor across open water to the other. She looked like a child trying unsuccessfully to do a chin-up. Her body was dangling below, and only by keeping her knees bent was she able to keep her feet above the swift water that was flowing underneath through the millhouse race. If the Widow lost her hold, she not only would fail to do her chin-up, she would plummet into the stream and float straight into the slowly moving mill wheel. Even the mountain wind whipping at the Widow's skirt seemed uncertain of the Widow's fate now.

With the Widow's danger evident, both boys went into action. "As light as she is, it'll still take both of us to pull her out," cried Paul. "I think I can jump all the way over. Then maybe between us we can work her up onto the board."

"Good," cried Ralph.

Paul jumped and managed, though barely, to clear the open water and land on the other side. Then leaning out

She would float straight into the slowly moving mill wheel.

over the plank he grabbed her hand in both of his own, and at about the same time Ralph from the other side took hold of her other hand.

Luckily the Widow was as light as she looked. Because it proved difficult enough, even with their help, for her to swing her body back and forth enough until finally she just managed to hook one leg up on the top edge of the floor on Ralph's side of the millrace. Paul, by walking on out on the plank, and kneeling, managed to shove a hand against the Widow just enough for her to roll up onto the floor and safety.

With surprising speed the Widow scrambled upright to her feet. Then she straightened her body to an erect position and at the same time began wringing water and mud from the lower part of her dress. "Wait till I get my hands on that Zeke boy!" she exclaimed. "Going all the way to the store for a dad-ratted stick of chawing gum at this time of night. Then first forgetting to tie that hold-to rope across the millhouse to keep me up instead of down. You talk about sense—"

"Is that the reason you fell?" asked Ralph quickly. "He forgot to tie a rope for you to hold to?"

The Widow gave him a quick glance. "You can say that again. He forgot it so he could go trotting off for a dad-ratted stick of chawing gum." Then she looked at Paul. "You look a heap more sensible up close than standing beside your dad, Cotton Top, talking about getting the law. And in case I forget to say it, I want to thank you and your friend here too. If it hadn't been for both of you, I sure would have drowned—and then some." The Widow turned and looked down into the millrace and shuddered. But then she again faced the boys, and she even seemed to smile at them, apparently because of being so relieved at her rescue. "Well enough of that. What's done is done."

"I'm sure glad we came along," Paul agreed. "We weren't sure—well, we weren't sure you wanted us, even when you called."

"Pshaw! When a person's life's in danger they don't have to be married to somebody to want help." The Widow straightened herself up even more, it looked like. "And just because I protect my property rights doesn't mean I'm not worth saving either, I might add."

"You've been good enough to let people come to work, all right," agreed Ralph. "And now this next Saturday we'll play Marble in the new building up the valley instead of at Marble."

"Provided you can do it without moving the water trough," said the Widow. "I grant I've bent a little by allowing folks back and forth past my place. But only because we had to have something to play basketball in. And because everyone's promised to stay flat-dab clear of that water trough going by."

"But why don't you want the water trough lifted?" Paul blurted.

"That's right," added Ralph. "My father knows how to build things, and he said you should move the trough higher up toward the waterfall, and you'd even get more water for your mill."

The Widow looked at one boy and then the other, and in the heavy shadows it seemed clear that she had stared across into the face of each for a while. Then she spoke, but as she did her voice seemed to have a strange new, faraway tone. "If you'll just follow me to the stairway landing, I'll show you something about that trough." Without waiting to hear their reply she began walking slowly toward the heavy door that Paul and Ralph first had opened upon hearing her cries for help. She opened the door with surprising ease, although it creaked on its rusty hinges as much as before.

Then she led the way outside to the old wooden landing at the top of the stairs. The boys followed, and to their surprise and pleasure found that the moon was peeking over the nearest mountaintop. It seemed to shine especially upon the water trough that sloped down to pass out of sight along the far wall of the millhouse.

Glistening in the moonlight on a level that was almost even with the boys' eyes, the trough somehow looked much less fearful than did its mossy, slimy appearance when viewed underneath as one walked by.

"My husband built that trough," she said, "with his own hands. Every piece of wood, every nail, every patch of tar. Fifty years ago he built it, too. Then one day it was done, and we looked at each other and both of us said, 'It'll stay in place as long as either of us lives. And when one of us looks at it, we'll remember the other. As long as it stands, we'll always be together.'" There was a sadness in the Widow's voice as she looked at the water trough now and sighed.

"But then the strip miners came, and they tore it down without a fare-thee-well. You think we could have stopped them? Once we tried, but those huge coal trucks—big as railroad cars—barreling down off that mountain makes you get out of the way real quick. Then they almost kept the stream dry using the water to wash the dirt off the coal. We couldn't work the mill because the trough was down, and there wasn't enough water in the stream. Before that we had the best mill in this part of the country. Raised our own corn. But the strip-miners ruined all that." The Widow pressed her shawl more tightly around her neck. "My husband was a kind and generous man. A great believer in law and order. That's what killed him, worrying over all that."

Suddenly she was a tired and lonely old woman. She began ambling down the stairs and across the walk to the cabin.

The boys stared after her as she departed. At last Paul spoke in a low voice. "So that's the reason," he said.

"Yes," Ralph said. "Can't say that I blame her for

protecting the water trough like she does."

"It makes a difference," Paul said, "when you know the real truth about something. The Widow doesn't seem so mean anymore."

Ralph nodded in agreement, and they resumed their walk on home.

Working Together

That day of the game with Marble Elementary was a day that many Kentuckians would long remember. It was a Fourth of July and Thanksgiving and Christmas all rolled into one. Paul's father asked in surprise why people in the Banks valley could get so excited about just one game. Paul's mother answered, "The people around here are starved for good news. So now when their elementary basketball team has a chance to win back a championship refused them last year—no wonder they're excited." Paul's mother, not much of a basketball fan herself, spoke of their team without seeming to remember that her son was on it. But at this stage Paul did not care who remembered what about his playing. He also was too excited, thinking about the game.

"The people around here are starved for good news."

It was someone's idea to have a pep rally at the feedstore gym and after that for as many as possible to march in front of the players' school bus as it drove up the hollow to the new gym. But first one thing led to another, and finally someone thought of having the small town band "go in front of the marchers who would march in front of the players' school bus going up the hollow." By the time this idea took hold, there were even some people with fiddles, and banjos, and guitars offering to march along and join the wind instruments

88

played by the various people around town.

So, on a sunny day in March, there they came—a very determined group parading gayly up the mountain road—their sounds echoing up and down the mountainsides. First came the cheerleaders waving their pompoms of purple and white, the school colors, and banners such as BE READY BANKS—OUTSHOOT MARBLE. Next was the band, its members dressed in everything from high school band uniforms to overalls worn by one older man who was playing a fiddle. Then came the noisy and dusty players' bus—running in low gear—and decorated with purple and white streamers. Next were the cars with horns blowing and children yelling. Behind them marched the people without cars and a few barking dogs.

Inside the school bus there was even more excitement. "At least they'd better not try and shoot the basketball out of the air like last year!" one of the players cried out from the rear of the players' bus.

"If they pull a gun, you won't stop them," Ken Kerr's voice mocked the speaker.

From beside Paul little Ralph Saylor, as usual, brought up a serious question, excitement or no excitement. "But what if we lose this game after all? Banks fans will commit suicide, won't they?"

"Ralph," Paul cautioned in a lower voice, "don't let anybody else hear you say that. Somebody might even think we wanted to lose."

As if taking the words out of Paul's mouth, Ken Kerr now called up his way. "Hey, ace, I don't hear you yelling. You sittin' up there, already countin' how many points you'll score yourself?"

"Yeah. I sure am. And I stopped counting at one

hundred," Paul called without bothering to look around. He tried not to let Ken's wisecracks bother him.

Several players must have heard both their remarks above all the noise, because there were quite a few laughs. But then suddenly Billy C., who was sitting on the front seat right across the aisle from Coach Bell, turned and gave Paul a hard stare. "You'd better not be counting to a hundred," he called back. "You'd better be thinking about passing the ball. Eh, boys?"

"I still don't think Billy C. would know a joke if he heard one," Ralph muttered into Paul's ears as elsewhere some laughs followed Billy C.'s words.

At this Coach Bell spoke. And it was straight at Billy C. "Let's nobody sound like a pot calling a kettle black. Anybody who knows anything about basketball knows that Banks Elementary doesn't pass enough. And that means everybody: our guards, our forwards, our centers. And if we don't get out there and pass that ball today, we won't come even close to beating Marble."

Coach Bell was getting warmed up to what he was saying, because now he even stood up and looked up and down the bus until he had looked at everyone. "As I've said before until I can hear myself saying it in my sleep, Marble's got a big bunch of boys on that team. And the only way for a bunch of fast smaller boys like ours to beat a bunch of big slower boys is to run them into the ground. And by that I mean fast breaks. And a fast break won't work unless you start throwing the ball fast, just about as soon as you catch it, and do it from the very moment we toss it inbounds from their end of the court."

Jerry Turner called up, "What happens, coach, if they pour water under our basket like last time just as someone comes racing down on a fast break and he slides into the end of the building and almost breaks his neck?"

"Yeah. What about that?" "What about that?" came calls toward the coach.

A frown crossed Coach Bell's face. "There won't be any funny stuff like that this time," he said, and his jaws looked hard as if he meant it. He sat down.

Several of the players were sticking their heads out the bus windows to get better views of the parade up front or the cars behind. Now someone pulled in his head and called inside the bus, "I see the Marble school bus bringing up the rear, way down the hollow."

"We ought to get out and throw rocks at them," someone else said, "like they did us last year."

Coach Bell made as if to turn around, probably to object to that kind of remark, but as he did so the band out front started playing something so loud and fast the coach only shrugged.

"They're playing, 'When the Saints Go Marching In,'" Ralph explained to Paul.

Paul listened. "It could be," he only half agreed because he was not sure. Anyway he already was beginning to think real hard about the game ahead, and for that reason was beginning to care less and less about thinking of anything else.

But suddenly Ralph spoke again toward Paul's ear, and what he said made even Paul forget the game. Or at least made him forget it for now. "This school bus won't go under Widow Stamps' water trough," he blurted. "It just came to me. It won't."

At first Paul could not believe what his ears were telling him. He just looked at Ralph and stared.

A sickening grin came to Ralph's face as he pondered what he himself had just said. "Aren't your dad and Coach Bell about the same height?"

"Of course they are—of course they are. But why?"

"Well—when your dad stands up in your house trailer his head almost touches the ceiling, doesn't it?"

"Yes. But what about it?"

"Didn't you notice Coach Bell just then? He stood straight up, and didn't touch the ceiling either. The same as in your trailer. Which means—"

Now Paul could only stare.

"Our bus is—" Ralph began again.

Paul's mouth went dry, but he managed to end Ralph's statement for him. "This bus must be as high as our trailer."

It was Ralph's turn to look at Paul without words. Then, at last, he muttered, "Hadn't we better warn Coach Bell?"

Paul considered this before shaking his head in the negative. "I don't think so. My mother always says, 'No use mentioning bad news unless we can change something.' And anyway—" Paul nodded toward the front windshield. "That thing ahead across the road the cheerleaders are marching under isn't some big mountain snake. We're almost there already."

Mr. Brown, the driver, must have started thinking about the trough also. Because even though they already were moving slow behind the people marching ahead, he began driving even more slowly, his eyes staring up toward the trough, coming ever and ever nearer now. Then abruptly Mr. Brown put his foot on the bus brake, and it came to a complete halt within a few inches of the trough. It was clear the bus could not go through without taking the moss-covered trough with it.

All the people had stopped now, too, and they were all looking toward the Widow's cabin. What's more, the Widow was on the porch looking at the bus. She stood there with her walking cane before suddenly disappearing into the shadows. When she appeared again, she held a gun instead of the cane.

"You see?" Ralph muttered into Paul's ear. "She's standing. And with that gun half-raised, too."

"I see," Paul agreed.

"And how can you blame her?" Ralph kept going on. "All of a sudden the Widow must see what looks like an

She stood there with her walking cane before suddenly disappearing into the shadows.

army come charging up the valley. You talk about noise and dust and people yelling and the band playing—and you know what that water trough means to her—well I just don't blame her for getting mad."

"I do," Paul said with impatience. "She had better not cost us the championship game."

Coach Bell had acted surprised like almost everyone else, but now he spoke to Mr. Brown. "This bus can't be that tall."

"I'm afraid it is."

Suddenly it became clear that the Widow herself believed it was that tall. And believed it very much. "The first person that touches that water trough," she yelled across the creek, in her surprisingly clear, loud voice, "is going to touch something harder than water. And I mean it too."

Coach Bell, whose shoulders today bore so much responsibility, stepped down from the bus, his heavy jaws firm in defiance. "We're on our way to the ball game, Widow Stamps. It's our championship game. With Marble Elementary."

"So. You want to play marbles, eh?" The Widow laughed at her own joke. "Well. This is no place to do it. This is private ground."

"Not this public road," Coach Bell objected sharply. He hesitated, then his attitude seemed to change because he smiled. "Billy C. Stamps and all the other players have been looking forward all year to this game, Widow. Did you know that?"

"Of course I know that. And I know you've got a good team, too." The Widow interrupted herself to stare toward the school bus, then said, "I don't reckon Billy C. is in that thing, too, is he?"

Coach Bell's smile grew. "He sure is," he said and nodded toward the inside of the bus. "Billy C. Come out here. I want the Widow to see you quick."

Billy C., never one to take orders if he could help it, did not respond to the coach's request. But the rest of the players had been hearing it all, and evidently they saw this as a good chance to get the bus moving again. They helped Billy make up his mind by pushing his reluctant body all the way to the doorway and on outside.

The Widow's eyes squinted against the bright sunlight. "That you, Billy C.?"

Billy C. hung his head in obvious embarrassment at so much attention.

"Your mind set on that basketball game, too?"

At this Billy C. looked up quickly, and his face brightened. "Yes'm. I sure am."

"Well, you're not the man my husband was, but at least you got his name. Which is more than most can say. I got a lot of corn to grind tonight. It's the biggest job I've had of late. The mill on the other side of the mountain has gone and broke down. If I can get this job out by morning looks like I'll be back in business. I can't come to the game and neither can Zeke—though he'll miss it sorely—so, Billy C., if I let this trough down, you boys better win." The Widow motioned her rifle toward the front of the bus. "Climb up there, and if you're man enough to lift it so the bus can go on through—well—I reckon maybe it just then can." Something about her own words amused the Widow, because she chuckled again. "Now get on up there, and do it soon."

Billy C. Stamps looked across at Widow Stamps

without seeming to understand. "If it's something that takes muscles, I can do it, Widow, but what is it again you want me doing?"

"Billy C., listen clear now. Climb up on the front of that school bus and see if you can hold that trough up for the bus, while the bus goes past underneath. You got it now, boy—you got it now?"

"I'll be glad to help him," interrupted Coach Bell and made a move as if to step that way. But the Widow had other thoughts and so indicated by motioning him back with the rifle.

"Hold it there. I said Billy C. Isn't nobody but a Stamps going to do it. Now move, Billy C. Get going, son." With this Billy C. moved. He kicked off his shoes and scampered up onto the hood of the bus under the trough. And he also indicated now that he knew what the Widow wanted him to do. The only trouble was, he tried and could not. He put both hands under the moss-covered trough and pushed up hard. But soggy and heavy from holding water for so many decades, it caused his hands to slip. The trough did not budge.

At the sight of her husband's namesake unable to lift the heavy, sodden trough, the Widow grinned and looked again toward the bus. "I reckon if all the players are in there, Cotton Top must be in there, too. Right?"

Coach Bell, before answering, glanced impatiently at his watch. "I don't know who you mean by Cotton Top, but it's less than thirty minutes before game time, Widow, and—"

Paul told himself at once, "I know exactly what the coach means about it being so late." He got up at once and walked to the front of the bus and on outside. There was little time left. "If you want me to try it,

Widow, I'll try it too. Because, like the coach says, we are running out of time." He slipped off his shoes also and—like Billy C.—he hoisted himself up without much trouble. How cold and damp and mushy the moss felt as he put his hands under the trough and tried to push up hard. And also how heavy. The Widow might have thought he was stronger than her namesake Billy C., but Paul soon discovered he was not strong enough. He knew all at once that he could not lift that trough alone.

"All right," the Widow said impatiently. "Now I want the whole team out on that bus, as many as can get on it, pushing up that trough. Get with it, coach, if you want to move on. I'm waitin'."

"What is this?" Coach Bell called. "Even if they lift it, what will they stand on while we drive the bus under it? It doesn't make sense. Not to me it doesn't."

But the eager players without hesitating came crowding out of the bus and slipped off their shoes and as many as possible climbed up on the bus hood. They also were aware that time was becoming a critical problem.

"You boys ought to be able to lift that," the Widow cheered from across the creek. "Now everybody lift at the same time and see."

As many as could reach up to it took hold of the bottom of the trough and began pushing upward. With a groaning noise, the trough began to give.

"Now you boys let it down," the Widow called, "so the end rests on that limb nearby."

They moved the trough over and up until the end came to rest on the limb. Bracing the end of the trough on the limb had raised it just high enough for the bus to squeeze underneath.

The Widow began to smile as the bus began to pull forward. She lowered her rifle so that the tip of the barrel rested against the floor of her cabin porch. "All right, folks," she called. "I just wanted to show you what working together can do. Even for a team—or I guess I should say—in particular for a team."

Everyone had turned now to stare at the Widow. She laughed again.

"So get the show on the road, folks. Hurry on up to that basketball game. We can't lose out two years in a row." She started inside her cabin, then turned and looked back. "One thing's sure, though. If you all don't win that game—that trough will be settin' down where it was—and your bus will never leave this hollow."

The Pine Needle

As basketball fans neared the new recreation building, a well-dressed man walked forward from a just-arrived helicopter. The man approached Paul's father, who was standing to one side of the throng entering the building. The newcomer shook hands with Paul's father as if he knew him, but at first the two men were too far away for Paul to recognize the man who had come in the helicopter. Then as the bus came nearer, suddenly Paul did remember him, after all. It was his father's boss, Mr. Randolph.

Now both men turned and observed the large crowd entering the building, and it was difficult to tell which of the two men looked most pleased, Paul's father or Mr. Randolph. The gym had done a good job of improving relations with the local people.

99

As the Banks' school bus inched forward through the crowd near the front of the building, the Marble school bus emerged from the valley behind. Ken Kerr pointed it out first by calling out, "All of us Banks players can run away now and hide. The bone-crushing Marble team is hot on our trail behind us."

"Is their tough-looking coach back there with 'em?" asked Billy C. "The one who looks like a bear wrestler."

Coach Bell, perhaps showing a strain of nervousness as game time neared, gave Billy C. a quick glance and also some quick advice. "Don't be worrying about their coach, Billy C. Instead, start worrying about his players—our opponents in this game."

The Banks' bus parked in front of the new building. Then the occupants, surprised, saw that a deputy sheriff waited beside the wide front doorway. In addition, freshly painted signs, tacked above the doorway, read: NO BOOZE ALLOWED INSIDE. NO GUNS ALLOWED INSIDE. It seemed clear that everything possible was being done to avoid the kind of trouble that had marred last year's game at Marble.

As Paul and Ralph Saylor stepped from the bus, both Paul's father and Mr. Randolph smiled toward them in recognition. Then Mr. Randolph motioned for the two boys to leave the group of players and hurry to them.

Paul, wondering if the coach might object, hesitated, but Ralph did not. "That's the big boss asking us," Ralph said. "Let's go see what he wants."

"Well, okay," said Paul as he looked for Coach Bell and was pleased to see him entering the building without noting the tardy players behind him. Ralph led the way toward the two men most responsible for this gym building.

"You boys should feel honored that Mr. Randolph is here on the day of such an important game," Paul's father greeted the boys.

"I'm here to bring you luck," said Mr. Randolph, and looked closely at Ralph and Paul.

"We sure need it," said Paul.

"We sure do," Ralph agreed.

"And I'll need luck in lowering the dam over the stream," said Mr. Randolph.

"The dam?" Paul asked.

"The dam?" Ralph asked also.

"Yep." Mr. Randolph grinned. "My contract with the state says I have to have the dam completed by midnight tonight. And with a half million dollars riding on this contract, I'm here to make sure there's no last-minute delays."

"But—" Paul began.

"But what about Widow Stamps?" Ralph completed for him and directed his question straight up to Mr. Randolph. "She's got to grind a lot of corn for someone this afternoon and tonight and if her mill won't run—"

"And she's moved the water trough so we could get the buses up the mountain," Paul said.

Mr. Randolph laughed. "When it comes to deciding between Widow Stamps and a half-million dollars, I don't have a problem in the world." He shrugged. "That dam has got to be lowered, or I will have broken my contract to reclaim this area."

Paul's father looked uneasily at the two boys. "I know you boys are concerned, but we have to do our job. We've got the frame for the dam ready. It's just a matter of dropping it in place, and Mr. Randolph says a helicopter is bringing it up in a few minutes."

The cheering inside the building grew louder. Suddenly a cheerleader appeared at the nearest side of the front door and looked out. "Coach Bell is asking for you boys. He wants you now."

"Oh yes," Paul said. "Sorry. We've got to run."

"Yes, hurry along," Paul's father said, and motioned for his son and Ralph to waste no more time. "The rest of our families are already inside. You sure can't hold up this game."

Paul and Ralph grinned a farewell and hurried away. But it was not a happy grin, and as the boys looked at each other they could see worry on each others' faces. Neither Mr. Daley nor Mr. Randolph had seemed to understand what would happen if there wasn't enough water to keep the Widow's mill running.

Just as Paul and Ralph approached the crowd gathered at the doorway, a man suddenly called, "Hey, officer. Arrest those two boys coming in the door!"

Startled, Paul and Ralph looked quickly, then recognized the man. They laughed. It was their own private coach Cliff Barnes, and Cliff's expression showed that he was joking.

"You startled us," Paul admitted. "Not that we've done anything to be arrested for, but this seems like the kind of day anything might happen, with everyone so excited and all."

Cliff continued smiling, but said, "You've done something wrong, anyway. You forgot this." He reached out and handed Paul a tiny object.

Paul hesitated, then took it. It was a pine needle. He might have expected this from Cliff. Paul looked up with a grin.

"Remember," Cliff advised. "A point nearest you on

the rim of the basket no bigger than the point of this needle. And just barely float the ball over the middle of it."

"And send the ball high up in the air," said Ralph and motioned with his hand in a high arc.

"High up in the air," Cliff agreed. He slapped Paul and Ralph in turn on the shoulder as they hurried past. "Now go in there and make up for last year," he said.

"Thanks. We'll try," said Paul.

"We sure will," Ralph agreed.

Increased sounds of excitement inside indicated the approaching game time. The band was playing and cheerleaders were leading cheers. Paul glanced over his shoulder and saw that his father and Mr. Randolph and Cliff and the others behind him seemed to realize this too. They were beginning to follow Ralph and himself through the doorway.

"Hey, Daley, hey, Saylor!" Coach Bell called as soon as he spotted them and at the same time motioned for them to hurry. "You boys are late. Get into this room behind me and change those clothes and get on out here."

Paul and Ralph broke into a run toward the room. As soon as they could they changed and returned to their coach and their teammates, all of whom were circled, luckily, under the nearest goal.

"You boys get in line—we're ready for warm-ups," Coach Bell ordered, his voice once more indicating his awareness of the approaching battle. The coach began directing passes to players as they rushed in under the basket, their basketball shoes squeaking against the new, shining oak floor. "This is a lot better than stumbling over that feedstore gym, isn't it, boys?" the coach

They seemed to be making a truly amazing number of shots.

asked, and his laugh may have been to reassure himself as well as the players. But the team was too busy trying to make their shots to reply.

It did not take the Banks people long to decide that Marble's team this year was the biggest elementary squad they had ever seen. Some of the Marble players were close to six-feet tall. Not only that, the Marble coach himself resembled the bear wrestler that Billy C. had suggested. He looked angry and determined, as if winning this game meant even more to his own pride than it meant to the Marble school players themselves.

And worse, the Marble squad began resembling the Harlem Globetrotters, so accurate were they with practice shots. Some of the players were even making them from near midcourt. When it came to practicing closer shots, including free throws, they seemed to be making a truly amazing number. Even their red-faced coach began to soften his expression some. He almost looked pleased as game time neared.

Coach Bell's team was just the opposite. The Banks basket seemed to have a blanket over it. Every now and then a shot would go in. But most of the time even the close ones would miss, circling the rim and falling off instead of rolling in. Coach Bell might try not to act worried, but it was obvious that he had a right to. His squad itself had a bad case of pre-game jitters.

Cotton Top

The referee whistled. As Coach Bell motioned his first team to huddle at the bench for last-second instructions before taking the court, Paul suddenly noticed one of the Banks fans leaving toward the front of the building. It was an unusual thing to do at this most exciting time, and Paul stared more closely. Then he recognized the man hurrying out. It was Mr. Randolph. Surely Mr. Randolph would wait until the end of the game before giving more thought to putting the dam in place. With misgivings Paul decided that Mr. Randolph must still be remembering the half million dollars. He possibly was even forgetting that the Widow was waiting down there to grind her corn.

Paul glanced toward the bench at Ralph, whose large eyes never seemed to miss much. Nor had they this time. Though Ralph was sitting with his back to the crowd, he also had glanced aside at just the right time to notice the departure of their fathers' boss.

Coach Bell noticed the pine needle that Paul was still clutching between a thumb and forefinger, and he laughed. "What are you doing with a pine needle, Paul? You can't play ball with that."

Slightly surprised, Paul handed the pine needle to Coach Bell.

"Sharp as a pine needle," the coach said and grinned. "That's what we are. All right—you boys here who are starting. Get out there and give them the needle." Coach Bell made an imaginary jab through the air with the pine needle that Paul had handed him. His gesture helped to relax things somewhat, and there were grins as the starters rushed onto the court. Cheers came from teammates who were not starting, and from the crowd that was more than ready for the game to start.

It was when the Banks players lined up with their opponents out on the court that they saw how really tall the Marble team stood. Tall in appearance and older in appearance also. It seemed really clear now that what many Banks fans had been saying was true. Marble Elementary must not be graduating its basketball players as rapidly as were some other schools.

Paul grinned as best he could as he glanced up at No. 23, the huge guard who was to be his opponent. The guard, redhaired and heavy-faced as was the Marble coach, also had the same kind of determined, unfriendly look as did the Marble coach.

Suddenly it became too clear that time for wondering was past. The referee tossed the ball. The centers jumped skyward. The championship action was underway.

As the centers reached up for control of the rising ball, Marble center No. 17 controlled the tipoff with surprising ease. The Marble center slapped it to Marble's No. 23, Paul's guard. The guard returned it to their center as they headed downcourt toward the Marble basket. And it was a good way to start the game, too. Good, that is, if you were a Marble instead of a Banks fan and wanted Banks to lose.

A Marble forward shot, but he missed. That, at least, was reassuring. Except that no sooner had he missed, and no sooner had the ball bounced off the backboard, than No. 17, the tallest player on the court—the Marble center—captured the rebound. He tossed it to their same forward who had missed the first time. This time the forward took more time. The ball went in. Clearly, with backboard support like that, any player on the Marble team eventually could rack up a score.

Paul found himself wondering why a team this good ever needed to earn a reputation for playing dirty, as Marble seemed to have. Certainly they did not need to play dirty now. Nor were they. Because they were such big boys, they were perhaps more awkward than smaller boys, but anyway here at the start they showed surprising skill at avoiding contact that might draw fouls.

Though Banks got the ball down to near their own basket, after that initial score by Marble it did them little good. True, Cully Apple managed a clean pass in to Billy C., but Billy C.'s shot fell far too short.

None of the other Banks players was doing much better. On one of those infrequent occasions when Paul found the ball passed to him instead of to Billy C., he was well-covered by his own tall guard, No. 23. Paul faked the guard out of position the first time and got into the basket area for a lay-up, which was Banks first score. But the Marble guard proved himself a fast learner, and the next time Paul tried this, No. 23 for Marble simply spread his legs and Paul found himself making his team's first charging foul. And a costly one, also. The guard made the free throw for still another Marble score.

Nor did Marble let up. Within the first few minutes of play Marble racked up three baskets and one free throw compared to the single basket for Banks. Marble led 7 to 2. It seemed clear that the size of the Marble players

Paul got into the basket area for a lay-up.

meant that Banks was in for a rough afternoon.

From the start Banks had trouble with its passing game. Or that is, with its lack of passing game. Cully Apple tried to pass to Billy C., but Marble's big center blocked that shot. Out of the scramble for the ball came Paul. He dribbled toward the sidelines and looked for a Banks player breaking for the basket. The only person who seemed open was Billy C. Paul hesitated. Out of at least a half dozen attempted baskets Billy C. had not scored the first one today. If only some other Banks player would break clear toward the basket. Paul faked, then dribbled aside, hoping to maybe drive toward the basket himself. But Marble's No. 23 was alert this time, skillfully keeping his body between Paul and the basket, forcing Paul to end his dribble. Paul must pass, though he was having trouble finding anyone to pass to.

"Hey, Cotton Top," Billy C. abruptly called out, his tone clearly angry. Toward Paul he trotted, arms forward, all but begging Paul to pass him the ball. "Hey, Cotton Top!" Billy C. cried, his angry face angrier. "That's what the Widow calls you, ain't it? Cotton Top? Throw me that ball."

Following Billy C.'s words, two things happened. First, Billy's words alerted the opposing center, and that center began guarding Billy C. even more closely. Therefore, Billy C. was no longer open for a pass. Secondly, and much more seriously, many of the Marble fans heard Billy C.'s words too, and they picked up the words joyfully.

"Hey, Cotton Top," one Marble fan yelled, his voice angry like Billy C.'s, though he did end his words with a roar of laughter. "Is that hair real, son? Is it really cotton, boy?"

Marble laughter grew, while another yelled, "Fancy pants hisself. Look at them cotton white shoes going with that cotton blond hair. Hey, neighbors, we got us a live one this time. Cotton Top hisself."

Whatever Billy C. had intended by using the nickname "Cotton Top," the results must have been worse than even he wanted. If he had wanted to poke fun at Paul in order to let off anger at not receiving a pass, he more than got even. The Marble fans seemed to think that by teasing one or more Banks players, it would make the entire Banks team nervous.

Paul did look different from any other player on the court. Not only was his hair a lighter color than anyone else's on either team, it was longer and thicker. It just so happened he was the only one with new white shoes, also, because his mother only last week had replaced his worn-out pair with these. And making Paul even more noticeable, he had scored Bank's only basket thus far in the game. If ever a player was a natural target for yells from another school, Paul Daley was it.

Making things worse, too, none of the Banks players had yet broken into the clear, though Paul was not clear to shoot and already had used up his dribble. So he was forced to try a desperate pass to Billy C., who at least was the tallest Banks player. However, the big Marble center batted Paul's pass aside, and a Marble forward came up with the ball.

In the scramble that followed, as both teams raced down toward the Marble basket, the Marble squad formed a good offense. By now the big Marble center was approaching the basket, and the ball came to him. He turned and flipped it in for a score. The Marble fans cheered more wildly than ever, because that basket seemed to break the game wide open for Marble. The fans began yelling "Cotton Top" as if they thought this had caused Paul to throw the wild pass that led to the latest Marble score.

Paul's face felt warm as more and more Marble fans yelled "Cotton Top" and other remarks poking fun at his hair or shoes. He could only hope that the sweat around his eyes was just that and no more—that it included no tears.

As the nervous Banks team tried to do something—anything—to move the ball in nearer the basket, Coach Bell's yells increased. "Pass that ball. Pass it around. They can't keep up with movement of a basketball. Pass it around."

After these called-in instructions, the two Banks guards did throw a few good quick passes to each other. But the passes failed to fake any Marble players out of position, and, in fact, they simply used up time needed by the Banks team in order to catch up on the sad-looking scoreboard that now read 11 to 2.

At least, however, while Marble stayed ahead with its scoring, Coach Bell's words did have some effect on Banks' passing attack. As the Banks squad passed the ball around more than any time so far in the game, the Marble squad itself for the first time seemed to act a little confused. Then Banks guard Sam Hughes suddenly saw an opening toward the basket, dribbled in, shot, and tallied. The way Banks fans cheered so loud after this second Banks basket, one might have thought that Banks now led 11 to 4 instead of trailed 4 to 11. At least Banks proved it had not gone to sleep entirely, though the first half ended, nonetheless, 11 to 4 in favor of Marble.

Coach Bell began yelling in from the sidelines. "Don't hurry those shots, boys. Start passing that ball! At least if we have it, they can't rebound it. Now pass that ball! Regain your cool, boys. Regain your cool."

Water Trough

It was a sad ball club that trailed Coach Bell to the Banks end of the court at halftime. Hot and much tireder than his part of the score would indicate, Paul walked with his gaze down, and so it was only from the corner of his eye that Paul suddenly saw Ralph motion toward the rear of the building. Paul looked up and followed Ralph's gaze. Ralph had motioned toward an open door marked "Exit" ahead behind the Banks' basket.

"I can't see the stream out there in back," muttered Ralph aside to Paul, "but I sure hope there's still enough water for the Widow's mill to run. I wish I could tell."

Paul looked toward the doorway and out across the land toward the stream. "So do I," he agreed.

Suddenly both boys noted a taller boy chasing a

smaller boy toward the stream. Then just as suddenly the smaller boy swerved aside, without any warning to the bigger one. More awkward, and with more height to manage, the taller of the two simply could not turn aside in time. Instead of stopping, his feet disappeared into the stream and its water shot skyward. At this sight the smaller boy, safely to one side, broke into loud laughter.

"We couldn't have had a better answer," whispered Ralph, unable to contain a quick laugh himself. "The water's still there. But shouldn't I go see Mr. Randolph and make sure? He has to know to leave the Widow's mill alone, because every other person in these mountains is related to her. Remember how only Cliff Barnes came to work, until the Widow gave everybody the word?"

Ralph alongside Paul was walking a little apart as the squad approached its halftime area. Paul tried to think quickly. There was barely enough time. "All right," he said then. "See if you can slip out into the crowd, Ralph, without the coach noticing you. If he does, I'll call to you, and you can hurry back maybe before he loses his cool."

"Got it," agreed Ralph and darted away through the crowd. Paul decided that being a second-stringer like Ralph maybe had one advantage after all. The coach was not waiting to bawl Ralph out during halftime, and so he might not be missed.

As it turned out, Coach Bell's pre-game nervousness had grown into disgust with his team's performance the first half, and he was thinking of nothing but that. "Does anybody here think we played good ball the first half?" Coach Bell asked and then turned abruptly and looked at Billy C. "Billy C., do you think we played good ball that first half? What's your truthful answer for that one now?"

When Billy C. only dropped his head, and none of the other players answered either, Coach Bell's expression seemed to grow a little less severe. "Well, now that everyone agrees it was a lousy first half, let's start thinking about the ballgame yet to be played. We still have a second half ahead of us. If a team couldn't come from behind, there'd be no reason for a second half. All right. Listen now. You boys can play better ball, and I for one know it. We've been doing one thing wrong all afternoon." Coach Bell pointed a harsh thumb toward Cully Apple. "You know what we've been doing wrong, Cully?"

Cully hesitated before saying sadly, "Everything, I guess."

"That's right," Coach Bell agreed, and in his case there was no hesitation. "But I'm thinking of the problem that's hurt us all season. I mean passing. Don't ever fail to look for somebody open nearer the basket when you're ready to pass. If one of your teammates is nearer the basket, then almost certainly he's in a better position to shoot. Paul Daley!" Coach Bell added sharply. He turned and looked at his blond-haired forward. "Don't let them rattle you, son, with that 'Cotton Top' garbage. I don't think they have, but they'll keep trying. You can depend on that. How come they started it, anyway, Daley? No other team has. You were on the far side of the court when it started."

"Well." Paul thought of looking toward Billy C., then something told him not to. If the coach was right, and what they needed was more passing, then what Banks needed was more teamwork, also. And it would not help any to accuse Billy C. of starting the name calling.

"Well, anyway," interrupted Coach Bell impatiently, "here's what I want you boys to do. I liked the way you faked your guard out of position on your first basket, Daley. And you can do it again—and the rest of you boys can do it also—if our team starts passing the ball. So right now I want to tell you two important things. We're going to do two things differently during the last half, and hear me out like your life depended on it, too."

Cully took this unfortunate moment to whisper something to Gerald Plank, and Coach Bell looked at both boys sharply. "Are you boys paying attention? I'm about to say something very important, so listen."

The coach glanced firmly around his group of players, and Paul was afraid he might remember Ralph. But Coach Bell seemed to be thinking of nothing now except what he had to say. "When a player has the ball, and he's not passing, I want you to remember something we learned from a lonely widow woman today. Remember what Widow Stamps said about pulling together to lift that trough? Lifting that water trough when it took half the team to do it? Well—remember also it's the same kind of teamwork on the court. It's not a one-man show."

Suddenly Coach Bell grinned. "If somebody has the ball and he's not passing, just yell out 'Water Trough.' Maybe that will wake him up." Coach Bell liked his newest suggestion so much, he stopped talking and looked around the group and continued to grin. "Yes, the more I think about it the better idea it is. I want to hear some 'water troughs' out there the second half.

Which brings us to this, a new plan for the second half. I'm going to try calling the shots for a while from the bench. Each of you boys knows your number. Billy C., you're No. 1; Paul, you're No. 2; and so forth. When you bring the ball down the court toward our basket, I want you to glance toward the bench and see how many fingers I have out. That will be your clue. One finger for No. 1; two fingers for No. 2; and the like. No. 1 means Billy C. gets to shoot; No. 2 means Paul gets to shoot; and so forth."

Cully Apple's flushed face grew a little redder now. He had been calling the plays all season, mainly calling all season for No. 1 which meant to feed the ball to Billy C. Now Coach Bell was taking over. But was it too late, Paul wondered. He hoped not. Of course he felt sorry for Cully, knowing as he did how much Cully enjoyed calling plays. Yet winning was of course even more important than Cully's play calling. Coach Bell must feel this also. At least he had an expression of confidence that he had not shown before he started explaining his plans.

"OK, boys. Let's do some warm-ups before the second half," Coach Bell concluded. "Remember what happened last year. They took it away from us then. Let's not leave any doubts about it this year."

There was handclapping among Banks players, and players slapped other players on the shoulders. "We'll do it." "Remember last year." "We'll do it, too."

As the two teams began warming up for the second half, Paul decided that he at least felt excited as everyone else. Also, he was doubly glad the coach had suggested the "water trough" cries. At the very minimum this could help drown out Marble's cries of

118

"Cotton Top" and whatever else someone decided to yell.

The referee was motioning for the starting teams to take their positions, but Paul found himself listening to the Banks cheerleaders who seemed best to be expressing the excitement he felt. They were yelling, "Coach Charlie Bell. He's our man. If he can't do it. Nobody can." As this yell ended, the Marble coach motioned to the referee and began asking him something. This had barely happened when Paul suddenly heard a familiar voice and turned to see a player approaching him. It was Ralph, returned from outside.

"What did you find out?" Paul asked quickly.

Ralph shook his head. "I couldn't find Mr. Randolph, but at least they haven't put in the dam yet."

"They haven't?"

"No. At least not yet."

"Well then. So far so good," Paul said.

Abruptly the referee blew his whistle. It was time for the second half. As the Banks players lined up with their opponents for the second-half tipoff, Paul hoped against hope that he would receive the tipoff and could race down the court and score. He hoped this even though Coach Bell had wanted to call the signals before each shot. But it was a wasted dream both his hopes and Coach Bell's. Because again the Marble center outjumped Billy C., and Marble got the tipoff ball with ease.

But unlike the start of the first half, Marble did not score right off. Instead, a Marble forward's shot for the basket tagged only the backboard. Rebounding for Banks was the other Banks forward, Gerald Plank. As

Marble did not score right off.

the Banks guards started up the court with the ball, Coach Bell gave his signal. He held up two fingers, which meant that he wanted Paul to take the shot this time.

For some reason, halftime instructions or no halftime instructions, Cully Apple chose to ignore Coach Bell's signal now that the second half had started. Cully must have seen it, though, because large-sized Coach Bell was easy to pick out among the players beside him on the bench, especially with two huge fingers jutting out over the top of his right knee. Cully, instead of passing to Paul, passed in to Billy C., as he had done during much of the first half. And, as in most of the first half, that tall Marble center was closely guarding Billy C.

"Water trough, water trough," Paul called out, suddenly remembering the coach's halftime instructions about Widow Stamps' words.

Billy C. did not act like he heard Paul's call. Instead he turned to shoot, stopping only when he found that the tall Marble center had him thoroughly blocked.

"Water trough! Water trough!" Paul insisted.

At last Billy C. could no longer ignore Paul's calling. He swung around quickly and shot Paul the ball. As a big and strong boy, Billy C. could throw unusually hard, and he may have put extra effort into his throw now. Or at least Paul thought so, from the way his hands stung when the ball arrived. But Paul tried to move quickly anyway. He faked, as if to dribble closer, and when his guard moved aside Paul raised his arms quickly and shot for the basket. The only thing was, though he shot for the basket he missed—and missed badly. He wondered if Billy C.'s hard pass had caused him to shoot too hard in turn. His shot had hit the backboard a foot higher than the basket, a poor reminder of all the practice time he had spent trying to improve his aim.

Paul's shot hit the backboard so hard it sent the ball rebounding out toward the middle of the court almost straight into the hands of Banks guard Terry Turner. At least Banks had recovered the rebound.

"Water trough, water trough," someone called. Paul looked toward that caller in surprise. This time it was the other Banks forward, Gerald Plank, calling the words, "Water trough, water trough." Beginning to grin widely, the usually quiet Gerald in fact called out still again, "Water trough. Water trough."

Terry tossed Gerald Plank the ball as requested, and grinning also now Terry himself suddenly called out "Water trough, water trough," thus asking for a return of the pass. Gerald did. Cully Apple suddenly laughed. He was getting the spirit of the thing too. "Water trough, water trough," he called over to his guard teammate. Cully Apple must have said the magic words as far as Terry was concerned. Terry shot his guard teammate the ball.

It was difficult to say now who was beginning to look more annoyed, the Banks center Billy C. or every player on the Marble squad. Billy C.'s annoyance may have been why Cully Apple ignored him now. At least Cully did now what he had not done, even when Coach Bell's two fingers had signalled him while ago to do so. He listened as Paul cried out again, "Water trough. Water trough."

Cully passed—a hard but good pass—not a rifle pass as Billy C. had thrown. Nor did Paul fake this time as if to dribble in. He did not have to. The Marble squad had grown so excited about all the unusual, unexpected razzle-dazzle by the Banks team, Paul's guard in excitement had almost backed to the free throw circle when the pass came sailing over to Paul. Paul took his time and wondered if Cliff Barnes was watching. He hoped so. He balanced the ball on his fingers, with his left hand under it and forward to guide it, and his right hand behind to propel it, as Cliff Barnes had shown him. "In other words, you're rolling the ball off the tips of your fingers," Cliff Barnes had said. Paul thought of the pine needle that Cliff handed him earlier today. He mentally laid the needle on the nearest point of the basketball rim and let the ball go. As the ball spun backwards off the fingers of his right hand, he tried to push it "higher than a kite" as Cliff had liked to say too.

Up it went and then down, down through the rim and on through the net, and the net barely moved.

Ordinarily Paul would not have felt so excited about a single basket midway in a game. But this one was different—it was the first real tryout of a new style of Banks play, to say nothing of a new kind of Banks team spirit. As the ball came down through the net, the excitement of it all hit Paul abruptly and he jumped off the floor, clapping his hands over his head. He could not help it, though after he did it he wondered if it might have looked a little funny. But no one acted like they noticed. The Banks fans appeared now to realize that this shot could be a turning point in the game. The Banks team had come out fighting to make the first basket of the second half. They had rallied to the clearly unexpected and strange cry of "Water trough." First one and then another of the Banks fans jumped up into the air. No longer did it seem to matter if a stranger in the community was the one trying to break this game wide open.

Paul looked toward the Banks fans, toward one person in particular. Yes, Cliff Barnes and no other deserved the applause now. There he stood—his powerful hands blasting each other in applause—the wide grin wider—his large freckles sparkling on his face. For an instant Paul's glance met that of Cliff's, and then Paul returned his attention to play. Groans from the Marble fans had been just as loud as the enthusiasm from the Banks side, and the Marble players, returning with the ball downcourt, were acting just as eager to change their own score now.

The Championship

If Paul thought that his making that last basket would get the Marble fans off his back, he found himself mistaken at once. "I'm gunning for you, Cotton Top!" someone yelled from the Marble side. "I'm about to pull me some cotton." Upon hearing that, and the responding roar of laughter from other Marble fans, Paul happened to remember the first thing he had heard upon coming here to Banks—about Marble shooting the ball from the air at last year's championship game. Well. If there was to be any gunning, he sure hoped they continued to shoot high toward a basketball, and not toward players or the crowd, including a player named Paul Daley, he reminded himself grimly. Although, of course, the deputy sheriff was here for this game, and people were on the lookout to keep law and order.

Hopefully that Marble fan had just been trying to rattle him. Paul determined to dismiss such dark thoughts from his mind, and did.

Downcourt Paul glanced at Billy C. For the first time this afternoon Billy C. had something of a smile on his usually sober face. Was Billy C.'s smile because of the threat from the Marble fan, Paul wondered. Did Billy C. still want so much to be the Banks star, he did not even like for his teammates to score, even in a championship game? Or was Billy C. also starting to catch the excitement of the other Banks players here in the second half?

The Banks squad perhaps grew overconfident too soon. A Marble forward broke for the basket and gained a step on Gerald Plank. The Marble center No. 17 passed to the forward, and the forward scored. Marble now led 13 to 6.

As the Banks squad returned the ball downcourt, Coach Bell again had two fingers forward. But this time the Marble guard No. 23 opposite Paul acted like he had learned his lesson. He was playing Paul tightly, with his arms moving up and down, acting very much like he expected someone to shoot Paul a pass. So Sam Hughes threw in to Billy C., instead, who swung around with the ball as if to make the same mistake again of trying to shoot over the top of the Marble center.

Paul saw Billy C.'s usual problem and called out, "Water trough." This time Billy C. seemed to realize it too. As Paul broke for the basket, Billy C. turned and blasted the ball Paul's way, as hard or harder than before. Clearly Billy C., for whatever reason, was trying to throw too hard. And again the pass had come so fast, Paul's guard was caught in surprise and was leaving him

A Marble forward broke for the basket.

open for a quick shot. He began dribbling instead of
trying to whip off a lightning-type shot. This not only
got him closer, but the action allowed his fingers to feel
normal again—to forget their tingling after that
unnecessary rifle shot from Billy C. Nor did he let it
bother him when, just as he was about to shoot after

*Paul began dribbling instead of trying to whip off a
lightning-type shot.*

dribbling, still another Marble voice yelled, "What's wrong, Cotton Top? That ball hit you like a bullet? Shake that hair up, didn't it now?"

Instead of it bothering him, it caused him to try even harder. As Paul stopped and leaped into the air to shoot, he imagined he was seeing the tiniest point of the tip of a pine needle. And he must have seen it, too. Because the ball again cleared the rim, and barely rippled the basket. As the Banks crowd roared wildly, the score on the scoreboard flashed to 8 points for their team. Banks now only trailed by 5 points, 13 to 8.

Paul's two baskets in a row quite clearly brought new life to the entire Banks squad. They could see the hopes rising on each other's faces as they began tracking the Marble players on their return down the court. They could hear it in increasing yells from Banks fans. All the Banks players seemed to move with more speed, like a bicycle speeding downhill.

As for the Marble players, Paul's two quick baskets seemed to have a bad effect on them. This became all too clear when even their tall center, so accurate in the first half, now missed an easy lay-up.

Sam recovered the rebound for Banks, and he and Cully passed it back and forth to each other on their way downcourt to the Banks goal. There could be absolutely no mistaking Coach Bell's signal this time. In addition to those same two fingers stuck forward, his heavy hands loudly slapped his knees excitedly to make sure he was being noticed. And to make sure that his guards heard him this time, he even called out loudly above the noise from the Banks crowd, "Play No. 2! Play No. 2!"

Now No. 23 guarding Paul began to treat him with

much greater respect. After all, Paul had just scored two baskets in a row from set shots, and the ball had barely ruffled the net each time. So the guard began playing Paul almost as closely as the Marble center was playing Billy C. Except for one difference. Whereas the Marble center had learned not to worry too much about Billy C.'s shooting, the guard opposite Paul had learned how dangerous it was to let Paul shoot.

So barely managing to hide a grin, Paul balanced the ball on the tips of his fingers as he had twice before in this half, and then he bent his knees as if to shoot. This was all the Marble guard needed. All and more. The guard's feet left the floor as if someone had pulled him upright by his own hair, and his arms shot upward in order to block the shot he felt sure was coming. Except that there was no shot. With his guard faked out of position—with his guard's feet off the floor—Paul found it easy to race around the guard, dribbling as he moved. His fake and run seemed to catch the entire Marble squad off guard, also. Not a hand touched Paul on his way on in to the basket. He leaped upward. It was an easy lay-up. Paul had now scored three in a row.

With Banks trailing by only three points at last, the Banks fans began to act as if the game was won. As for Marble, fans as well as players began to look toward Paul with more respect. The "cotton top" with the white shoes no longer seemed as funny as in the first half of the game. Those three quick baskets by Paul had somehow made it less funny to call him names.

Banks was on the move, like a train racing on a straight track. This successful second half for Banks began causing Marble players to play even more roughly, now that Banks was getting better. But as Marble played roughly, Banks played skillfully. Banks players had reason to remember Coach Bell's favorite expression, "When the going gets tough, the tough get going."

No. 23, guarding Paul, began to look angrier than ever. The fact that Paul had faked him out of position so completely on that last Banks basket had not made No. 23 happy at all. Evidently to get back at Paul, No. 23 began playing him even closer. In fact, the Marble guard was now playing him so close, there were times when Paul could see nothing except No. 23's red hair and tight mouth. He could even feel No. 23's hot breath on him.

It was difficult to get the ball now to Paul, even though Coach Bell was beginning to push two fingers so far over his knee they looked like the forks of a slingshot strapped to his leg. Seeing that Paul was covered so tightly, Cully Apple in the excitement took a longer shot than he was supposed to. He let the ball go before he was fully set, and it was a poor shot. Instead of the ball floating over the basket rim, it hit the front of the basket and bounced straight up into the air. Yes, it was a poor shot except for one thing: after the ball bounced straight up, it of course came down. And when it did it hit the inside of the rim and began rolling around and around and around until finally it settled inside for the score.

It made no difference that Cully's shot had been a lucky one. Certainly it seemed to make no difference to Banks. Cully and other Banks players began jumping up and down and clapping hands as if he had made a set shot from midcourt. And one thing was sure. The score on the scoreboard changed just the same. Banks was now trailing by only one point. Cully had broken his

It began rolling around and around inside the rim.

habit of passing mainly to Billy C. and had made the most exciting shot thus far in the game.

Marble players and fans saw nothing lucky about Cully's shot. It was unlucky for the score and for their team spirits as well. Their ball handling began to look like the poor playing shown by Banks the first half. Some of their passes became careless, and when a pass came toward the player guarding him, Paul saw it coming in time to intercept it. When this happened, the player guarding him, No. 23, showed similar carelessness. He all but jumped all over Paul in order to wrestle the ball from him. Marble fans applauded wildly, and Banks stood up in a group, booing in protest.

But Marble's mistake proved serious. The referee blew his whistle.

"Foul. One shot!" the referee cried, and to make sure there was no mistaking it he extended a hand high and held up one finger. The referee strode firmly with the ball toward the Banks foul line. Paul was glad that no one knew how wildly his heart was pounding inside his hot, sweaty body as he followed the referee. He wanted to look toward Cliff Barnes, as he had done earlier in the game, at a time that had worked so well. But no chance now. He was being offered a quick chance to tie the score, and there was time to think of nothing but that. Instead, when the referee handed Paul the ball, he bounced it a couple of times on the floor as Coach Bell had taught all the squad to do. This was to help relax his muscles. Then he prepared to try for a tying score.

Paul did not think about his muscles now. He did not consider whether bouncing the ball had relaxed them, or if it had not. Instead he thought again of that imaginary point at the basket. He could not afford to take the chance Cully had taken and have the ball bounce high into the air. He put his right foot forward. He rested the ball on the tips of the fingers of his right hand and held it there with his left. It was a high arc and straight and true. Most Banks fans seemed to know he had done it even before the ball floated over that nearest point on the nearest part of the basket.

In the rush of noise that followed, Paul realized only one thing. He realized it without even looking at the scoreboard. His free throw had tied the score, 13-all.

For the first time in the game Banks was not behind.

The rest of the game was almost like a dream, as far as Paul felt. The score see-sawed back and forth. It did not seem important to Paul that he and others had made more baskets. He just knew that Banks must win. The score on the scoreboard climbed to 20-20.

The scoreboard clock showed only 30 seconds remaining in the game. Banks had possession of the ball. Coach Bell called time out. As the Banks squad hurried toward their coach, Paul blinked his eyes. He was back to thinking clear facts. The next few moments would prove for good championship in these Kentucky hills.

Coach Bell did not begin with his usual time-out pep talk. "Boys, I've decided not to call this last shot myself. If you're clear and think you can make it, then take it. It's that simple. There's too much noise, too much action, too much confusion, too much excitement for any human to call it now from the bench."

After the coach's words, there was sudden silence. Then Cully Apple blurted, "You mean anybody can shoot that's open?" When he asked this, Cully did not look at Billy C., but it seemed clear that he was surprised the coach was giving Billy C. any chance at all to shoot again. After Billy C.'s lousy shooting in the first half.

Coach Bell nodded his head with firmness. "Absolutely anybody." Then, as if to answer Cully's unasked question, he added, "They've been leaving Billy C. open. If they pull it again, and you have a clear shot, Billy C., take it. And you other players, too." Coach Bell paused, and then said with soberness, "This game is now your game, boys. No coach can win it for you from here on out. It's up to you, and you, and you, and you.

It's your decision now whether to win, lose, or draw."

When the coach finished speaking, Paul's glance happened to cross Billy C.'s. Paul decided to speak to him. "If you're open, take it, Billy C., and win the game for us," he said.

Billy C., instead of answering, looked away. Paul decided that Billy C. thought he was trying to boss him, which he had not meant at all.

The referee blew his whistle. As Paul hurried out onto the court, he happened to see the front door of the building open and Mr. Randolph return. Strangely, though Mr. Randolph still wore his business suit, there seemed to be grass or weeds clinging to one leg of his suit trousers. Did this mean that Mr. Randolph had been working at the dam? Could it be that only the increasing excitement here near the end of the game had brought him in to watch the final moments of play?

Cully threw in from the sideline. He threw it straight to Paul. Paul turned to dribble closer, but the Marble guard was playing him too skillfully. Paul must either pass or shoot. He tried to tell himself to shoot, that he had to make it. But he was too far out. What if he missed? Paul glanced at the clock. Ten precious seconds of the fading thirty seconds were already passed. Twenty seconds remained. The coach had taught them to wait until the last few seconds to shoot. That way, if you missed, the opposing team would not have time to score.

None of Paul's teammates was in the clear. From the corner of his eye Paul glanced at Billy C., but Billy C. did not appear to be trying very hard to break into the open. The referee's back was turned briefly to Billy C., and the big Marble guard took this opportunity to shove an elbow roughly into Billy C.'s side. Evidently Billy C. was having problems in more ways than one.

"When the going gets tough, the tough get going," Paul reminded himself. He mentally wished Billy C. luck. The clock showed ten seconds. Paul prepared to shoot. Except that the huge Marble center could see the clock also, and he also knew that Paul must act and do so now. The big center leaped toward Paul, and so now, in addition to Paul's guard, the Marble center also was guarding him. It was a classic two-on-one situation with Paul trapped and time running out, the game slipping from his grasp.

Except that a Banks player suddenly raced nearer Paul and yelled, "Water trough." Paul, in amazement, recognized the voice and the player. The voice and words were Billy C.'s.

Paul felt his heart jump as he took this final opportunity to get rid of the ball. He passed to Billy C. Billy C., with ball raised, turned ready to shoot. But Paul now did as Billy C. had. He raced for daylight, and the daylight happened to be toward the basket. The two Marble players who had been guarding Paul then jumped to keep Billy C. from shooting, leaving Paul even more in the open. Thanks to their eagerness—Paul found himself wide open as he neared the basket.

Billy C. Stamps looped Paul Davis Daley the ball with three seconds showing on the scoreboard clock. Paul caught it and made an upward leap, and as Paul's feet left the floor, so did the feet of many of the Banks fans. "As easy as taking candy from a baby," he told himself, in order to be relaxed, and at the smae time doing his best to fight back the tears.

As the ball bounced off the backboard and down

Paul caught it and made an upward leap.

through the hoop, winning this championship game for Banks, Paul's feet landed on the floor. But they did not seem to land. Instead he felt like he was floating as the hands of his teammates began to slap against him in praise. Paul looked around. Billy C. was clapping harder, or almost, than any two other boys. Billy C. no longer was calling him "Cotton Top" or making fun of his white shoes. Instead Billy C. cried out, "Water trough!" Paul nodded—brushing the sweat—or was it tears—from his eyes. It was hard for him to talk just now.

"It was a rifle pass," Billy grinned. "But you caught it."

Coach Bell and the other players and the Banks crowd were now gathered around the tired but victorious Banks players on the court. "That's the way to pass and shoot," Coach Bell started saying again and again until he interrupted himself to add, "That was the prettiest lay-up I ever saw, Paul. You were alone—wide open and alone."

"Because of the pass," Paul said.

Coach Bell looked at Billy C. "And because of the passer," he added.

Paul laughed. "Billy C. was even yelling 'water trough' at the end. Somehow it sounded a whole lot better than Cotton Top, didn't it, Billy C.?"

Billy C. nodded, and laughed with Paul.

A Stall For Time

In the excitement of winning the championship, it was easy to forget the Widow and the stream. But once outside the building used for the gym, Paul and Ralph saw something that reminded them of her and it. Among some men near the dam area stood their fathers and Mr. Randolph, and Mr. Randolph was looking very pleased. The dam was in place and the water in the stream below the dam was not.

"Ralph!" cried out Paul. "They've already got the dam in place. I'll run down to the Widow's and see what's happening and come right back to Mr. Randolph. He'll just have to change his mind."

"Okay," Ralph replied as his friend began hurrying toward the line of pickup trucks, cars, and people that were jamming down the valley.

The workers at the dam had been wearing hard hats, and Paul believed that on ahead down the hollow he could see their truck moving slowly in the procession. It was a slow-moving line, and suddenly Paul found himself running alongside an old car crowded with men and women and children. The driver was wearing a steel hat. Paul slowed and called in through the open window to the driver. "Were you working on the dam?"

As soon as the driver turned his face, Paul saw his mistake. The driver had a lamp on the front of his hat. He was a miner.

"Nope," the driver said.

Paul was about to thank him and hurry on but suddenly, from the crowded back seat, a woman's voice called out, "Hey, ain't you the boy that won that game for Banks?"

Paul stared. Something about her tone made him hesitate to answer.

The woman spoke again, and this time her voice clearly sounded shrill with anger: "You is, and so get them dirty hands off this clean car, son. That was a lucky shot if I ever see' one. Banks didn't no more deserve to win than—"

Paul left them at once, telling himself that he had no time now to talk about the game.

He made his way through the lines of people walking at a slower pace and at last found himself nearing the rear of a truck carrying a group of men seated on benches and wearing hard hats. Paul called, but they were talking excitedly to each other and he could not get their attention above the noise of the truck. So he ran on until he was trotting alongside even with the driver.

"Aren't you the men that were working on the dam?"

"And aren't you Paul Daley, the boy who scored that winning basket?" the driver called out with a sudden wide smile.

"Yes," Paul said hurriedly and returned the smile the best he could while breathing dust and exhaust fumes and running beside the truck and trying to let his dry voice talk without rasping, all at the same time. "Can you people go back and—help with another job?"

"Do what?"

"Help with another job." Paul could not explain it all now, and besides they might not understand the importance of it. "If you could go back—go back—"

"In this traffic?" The driver glanced at his rearview mirror, and his smile faded. "Nobody could turn a truck around in this traffic and head back up that hollow. Don't you see that crowd behind us, Daley?"

"Don't you see that crowd behind us, Daley?"

"I know. But when you—when you get to the mill, just stop and wait—"

"Son. These fellows have chores to do at home. They're already running late. I'm sorry—no, I couldn't."

It was strange, Paul thought, that a minute ago the driver had been so friendly and bragging about his winning a game. Now, when a favor was asked of him, his smile seemed to go away pretty fast.

"Thanks anyway," Paul called over his shoulder and was already leaving the truck behind. In fact, he no longer was worrying about the driver or the truck. He was thinking about what he would say to Widow Stamps.

When Paul took the time to look at the lowered stream, it seemed to be flowing so slowly it was almost

"Thanks, anyway," Paul called over his shoulder and was already leaving the truck behind.

still. He wondered if the water was even high enough to touch the mill wheel.

As he neared the millhouse, Paul crossed his fingers in hopes that the big load of corn the Widow was to grind into meal had not arrived. He raced ahead and then left the road and crossed the wobbly stairs into the millhouse. Sure enough, there was the Widow, getting ready for her customer and about to discover that the water was too low to turn the wheel. The old lady's shawl was hanging back toward her shoulders, and her large brown eyes were clear and excited as she turned and gave Paul a surprised look.

The Widow recovered herself quickly, however, and greeted him. "What a pleasant surprise, Cotton Top. Since I'm not about to drown, or anything, I bet you won that game, and I reckon you wanted to be the first to tell me."

"We sure did." He returned her smile. He never did mind that she called him "Cotton Top." But then his smile faded, and he pointed toward an open window facing upstream. "Do you see what's happening, Widow. They've lowered a dam at the recreation site. And that's all that's left of the stream." Paul was right. Already the water was so low it did not touch the mill wheel.

The Widow turned and looked. Her frail body jerked more quickly than ever Paul would have thought possible. "Oh no!" she cried. "You mean they're stopping my stream to build 'em a lake up above?"

"But only for a little while, Widow. I'm going to ask them to open the dam," he said hurriedly. "You see it was in the contract. The dam had to be ready by midnight tonight or Mr. Randolph and my dad and Ralph's would be in trouble. I'm going to get them to open it—I'm going right now."

"Trouble? What do you all know about trouble? This job's the first chance I've had in years to get this mill back on its feet since my husband died. I had to go and get soft in the head and let you move that trough. Zeke!" With a quick turn she grabbed a rope that went up to the ceiling, through a pulley, and out a hole to the outside. Paul could hear a distant bell clanging from the cabin. And in seconds he could hear the loud rumbling of the swinging bridge.

Then Zeke came in, his one eye focused on the Widow as if he did not know Paul was there.

"Zeke," she said. "I'm about to have you set that water trough back where it was. You hear me now, boy?"

Zeke nodded and still did not look at Paul.

"But, Widow," Paul interrupted. "What about the people still leaving the game—I mean the buses might not be past yet."

"As I say, this trough is on private property, and so is this mill. I've got a going business and a customer coming on." She turned and faced the disappearing water and laughed bitterly. "That stream down there sure's not enough to turn this wheel!" Again she commanded, "All right, Zeke—"

"But one final thing, Widow," Paul interrupted again. "Don't you really think you owe me something? I hate to mention it, but you know—" Paul looked toward the plank across the millrace where he and Ralph had pulled the Widow up that day. Then suddenly he had a second idea, and he faced the Widow with a new fresh smile. "It was what you did that helped us win that game. I forgot to tell you. We all remembered how you had us working together to lift the trough, and so we just started working that way on the team—and we began yelling 'Water Trough—Water Trough'—" Paul found himself feeling excited even just telling it—even just remembering it— "And Billy C. himself started yelling it and threw me the pass that won the game and—"

"Billy C. started playing ball just like anybody else?" the Widow asked quickly.

"Yes," Paul said, feeling at last that he was making headway with the Widow and deciding to make even more. "Billy C. threw me the pass that let me make the basket that won the game, and do you know who was the first person to slap me on the back as soon as it went through—it was your nephew, Billy C.—he was the first, he sure was—and—"

"Do you hear that?" asked the Widow brightly, looking at Zeke. "Billy C.'s learning how to get along with his fellow man. OK, Zeke. I don't know what I'm raising you for except to do as I say—so go out there now to that trough and do—"

"But, Widow," Paul said desperately. Quite clearly his good words to her had not changed her mind. "What if I promise, and I mean absolutely promise, to have that dam opened up before nighttime comes?" Paul did not know how he could do it, but he did know he had to say something to make her agree to give him enough time. If Zeke put that trough back the way it had always been, things would be just the same. Always a battle every time anything bigger than a car tried to come up the valley. Besides he knew, just like everybody else, the road did not belong to her, and with the government owning the strip mining area, they could condemn the water trough whenever they took a notion. But that was not the way to do it—not with what the trough meant to her, the way she and her husband had built it.

The Widow must have noticed Paul's earnestness, now, because when she looked at him she looked for a long time and then her expression softened some. "You sure are a talker, aren't you, Cotton Top? You keep on a trail like a hound I once owned. Well—I don't know." Slowly the firm lines of her tiny body relaxed. "Well, Cotton Top," she said. "Well, now—you absolutely sure you can make those crazy builders get sense in their head 'ere evening comes? Actually I guess I could grind that meal in an hour—providing worst comes to worst."

The Widow had been honest and helpful all along. She had showed them how to work together with the water trough. Paul had to be honest with her too. "I think we have just as much chance to open that dam as we had to beat Marble—when everybody said we'd have so much trouble. And you helped us do that. That's why I think you'll help us now.'"

She turned to Zeke. "You remember Brute, don't you, Zeke? My hound that never stopped?"

At last Zeke grinned and looked at Paul.

"He never gave up," the Widow continued. "I'm surprised now we didn't call him Cotton Top, instead. Well, OK. I'll buy it, I guess." The Widow's frail body straightened with new determination. "Zeke, you run along here with Cotton Top, just like it used to be with Brute."

Zeke needed no further orders. He began trotting out the door toward the road as if the hound were already on the chase. Unwilling to chance the Widow changing her mind, Paul also acted quickly now. He said,

"Thanks," and began following Zeke at once. If the Widow wanted to think of him as a hound, he deserved it, Paul decided. His father had certainly brought her enough trouble into this hollow.

The Full Team

Running behind Zeke took a lot more energy than Paul would have thought. But at least one thing was sure. It felt better running behind Zeke than having Zeke running behind him.

As they made their way up the road through the dwindling crowd, Paul was recognized by first one person and then another. "Hey, champ. Great ball game," someone greeted him before he hurried past, and to save his breath he simply smiled in return. Another greeted him with, "We sure won that one, didn't we, Paul?" Paul nodded but again only smiled, because Zeke sure was setting a fast pace. No wonder Zeke gave him and Ralph such a chase with that axe, Paul reminded himself with grimness now.

Just as they reached the parking area of the new gym

someone in a pickup truck pulled in front of Paul and
Zeke.

"Hey there!" a familiar voice shouted, "who's chasing
whom?"

Paul stopped short and looked up in the cab at the
smiling face of Cliff Barnes.

"Cliff—" Paul fought for breath. "You gotta—help."

"What's this?" Cliff said, jumping out of his truck
and looking at Zeke who had gone about a hundred
yards on and stopped. "Zeke bothering you again?"

Paul shook his head. "No. It's the Widow."

"Is she hurt?" Cliff was about to get back in his
truck, but Paul touched his arm.

"Wait a minute," Paul pleaded. "It's just that I'm so
out of breath." While Paul tried to calm his breathing,
Cliff put an arm around his shoulder. "That sure was a
great game. I'm proud of you."

Paul nodded, able to talk now. "They lowered the
dam," he said, pointing to it.

"Yeah, I helped," said Cliff.

"The Widow moved the trough, too, and she's got a
customer from the mill across the mountain—it's broken
down—and she's got to do the job tonight or they'll take
it somewhere else. It's her big chance to get back in
business."

"I see." Cliff nodded. "And she doesn't have any
water power to turn the water wheel, of course?"

"That's right. You got to help us, Cliff. You just got
to!"

Suddenly Cliff pointed to the dam. "I don't know
who is most concerned about the Widow, you or Ralph.
But if you hadn't been running after Zeke so hard and
had taken time to notice, you'd see that dam's opened

up and the water's flowing through full strength. In fact, the Widow's probably wishing Zeke was back there helping her get started." Cliff motioned for Zeke to come toward him. "Everything's OK," he said, and pointed toward the stream. "You better go back and help at the mill."

Zeke had just headed down the road as Ralph, Mr. Daley, Mr. Saylor, and Mr. Randolph came walking up.

"Let's go, son," Mr. Daley said. "We're going down and fix that water trough now, for good."

"That's right, son," added Mr. Randolph. "Ralph explained everything, and I have to admit all the contract said was we had to have the dam in place by midnight. It didn't say a thing about the lake being full, so we'll just let the water run through until we can build that water trough right."

Paul realized that he was being nudged by someone beside him. It was Ralph.

"Hey, champ," Ralph said. "We did it, didn't we? We got the mill wheel turning again."

Paul looked at little Ralph's large blue eyes behind the thick glasses. "You're the champ, Ralph. You're the one who made the score this time."

"No, not just me. It took us all. Just like your winning the game. I mean, our game."

"Yes, it did take us all. Our dads and Mr. Randolph for the gym, the Widow for lowering the water trough, Billy C. and the team—"

"Don't forget me!" said Cliff Barnes.

"Most of all you!" Ralph said, nudging Paul again. And Paul, very plainly remembering the day Cliff had saved them from Zeke's axe, and the way Cliff had so patiently taught them to shoot a basketball, chimed in with Ralph. "Most of all you, Cliff!"